CW01024500

Hello, I'm Your Polish Neighbour

All about Poles in West London

Wiktor Moszczynski

AuthorHouse™ UK Ltd.
500 Avebury Boulevard
Central Milton Keynes, MK9 2BE
www.authorhouse.co.uk
Phone: 08001974150

First published by AuthorHouse 01/04/2010

ISBN: 978-1-4490-9779-0 (sc)

This book is printed on acid-free paper.

I would like to take this opportunity to thank the Polish Ex-Combatants Association (SPK) in Great Britain and the Polonia Aid Foundation Trust for their generous contributon to the cost of publishing this book, as well as to the Polish Embassy for both their material support and for promising to allow me to use their premises to launch the publication of this book.

Author

Surviving a Polish Christmas

We all have the post-Christmas blues now. Remorsefully we nurse our empty pockets, our mounting credit card bills, our bulging tummies ("Speak for yourself!" says my 16-year old son) and our discarded Christmas trees lying in the garden as we gather the energy to carry them to an approved council disposal site.

If you're Polish you experience this with even more intensity. Poles of all generations take their Christmas seriously. Especially when abroad. They miss their families and friends in Poland, their toboggans in the snow and their childhood memories of meeting St Nicholas (that's Santa to our British friends) on 6th December, when they got their Christmas presents early. Yes, kids! Your Polish school mates get presents TWICE at Christmas; once on St Nicholas' day and once at Christmas. Very sneaky. I bet they did not tell you that!

So to compensate for these dreams of childhood, Poles in Ealing spend twice as much at Christmas, consume twice as much food and drink, and exercise twice as much by walking to the Polish church at Windsor Road to sing their carols lustily to the rooftops and show off their presents to each other.

The big event is Christmas Eve which is the last day of the pre-Christmas fast. This fasting takes the form of a 12 course meal. Strictly only fish, vegetables and fruit; but mountains of it! Beetroot soup with dumplings alternates with mushroom soup; herring swimming in vodka is followed by carp petrified in aspic; pasta with poppyseed alternates with dried fruit compotes. Before the feast (sorry, the fast) begins, everybody, young and old, arm themselves with holy wafers and then they proceed around the table ensuring that everyone has broken bread and hugged and kissed with everyone else present, wishing them success and health in the New Year. Poles are traditional huggers. After that, the kids open their presents under the Christmas tree, the energetic go to midnight Mass and the elderly sleep it off.

Until the next day, when… When we all suddenly go English, and stuff ourselves stupid with turkey or goose and all the usual roast trimmings. After all, we had fasted the night before!

Ealing Gazette January 12th 2007

Courtfield Luncheon Club

You can see them outside the Polish Catholic Centre on Windsor Road. They come by community buses, or with relatives by car. Most come proudly on foot. You could easily miss them. There are distinguished gents with wisps of white hair peeking under their berets greeting ladies with beautiful faces creased by the wrinkles of time and experience, pocketing their orange bus passes as they descend off the 207 bus.

These are the old guard, survivors of German camps and Siberian wastes, veterans of Normandy and the desert campaign. They are the distinguished remnants of the old Polish community visible in Ealing over the last 50 years. Their host, Bohdan Mordas, greets them respectfully.

Every weekday they can come here to attend the Courtfield Social and Luncheon Club, where they enjoy the international cuisine cooked on the premises. They come to chat, read Polish and English magazines, reminisce about pre-war Poland, complain about modern Poland and catch up with the gossip. Those who have families can boast about their children and grandchildren or console each other over their illnesses and arthritic limbs, while the ladies surrender themselves occasionally to the luxuries of a visiting beauty expert.

Wednesday is the special day. Wednesday is the day that a youthful professional trainer, Jolanta Potocka, exercises them to the sound of dance music. Then up go those weary limbs as the elderly gents stretch their shoulders and necks, and vie with each other to impress their demanding mistress. There is spirit yet in those seemingly fragile bodies. The same spirit that kept them going through the Gates of Hell during wartime and now recharges their batteries as they survive another winter's day in Ealing.

This Social Club is not exclusively Polish. There are many nationalities here, including English, sharing their comforting warm meals. It has served some 10,000 meals every year for over 30 years and received an annual grant from Ealing Council (until now), as well as a subsidy from the Polish parish in the free hire of the hall. At their Christmas party in December, Mrs Diane Pagan, the Mayor of Ealing, shared in the festivities and thanked the voluntary community workers running the Club for their contribution to the people of Ealing.

Ealing Gazette January 19th 2007

Beneath the Windmill

The noise was deafening and circling strobe lights blinded me while lighting up the crowded interior. I looked for a free seat. There was one at a table with 3 Polish skinheads. I sat down and plonked my pint of Tyskie beer on the table, gingerly.

The lads were actually quite shy but ready to chat to a fellow Pole. They came from a small town in the foothills of the Carpathians. Now they lived in a poky flat in Watford where they worked as cooks and kitchen porters. Piotrek had just had his 27th birthday and I drank his health. If David Cameron can hug a hoodie then I can drink to a skinhead. Apparently they came here often for the best Polish disco night in West London.

The Windmill on Acton High Street is a traditional Irish pub but its large back room is used for Polish disco nights on Sundays. There is no entrance fee. The young faces around me were relaxed and joyful. Their day jobs as cleaners, secretaries, waiters, motorbike riders were behind them. Their dismal flats in Greenford, Feltham and Shepherds Bush awaited them. Here they were kings of the dance-floor, drinking with their mates or flirting with the very friendly Polish female talent around them. There were some 120 people in the room and the bar was busy, but everyone I spoke to said this was a quiet night. Not everyone had come back from their family Christmas reunions in Poland yet. By February there would be twice as many.

The place seemed safe. An underage youngster without an ID was turned away at the door. A scuffle was sorted out with a prompt ejection of the main offender by bouncers.

Wicek Batyma, the 33 year old DJ, was alternating Polish 70s ballads with rock numbers and Shakira. No frenzied dancing here; no disco polo. "It's vacation type music", he explained, "Polish Karaoke." Just then he played the popular "Agnieszka doesn't live here any more" and a crop of Polish girls started leaping up and down like Masai warriors. The guys stood back. They still had their beer to quaff and the warmer socializing could follow later. For instance, on the night bus going home.

Ealing Gazette January 26th 2007

The Children of Solidarity

The 30 year old construction worker drew himself up, his face betraying anger and bitterness. "Then they told us," he continued in Polish, "we would be better paid at a further site 10 miles away. Less skilled workers would replace us at the first site. So we went there. Three days later, they told us, there's no work for us at the new site. We had simply volunteered ourselves into redundancy." These and similar tales of woe were poured out to Community trade union officials at a recruitment meeting in the Polish Social and Cultural Centre in Hammersmith.

Another Pole complained that he had been sacked just before the first year of his employment ran out so that he would be unable to benefit from a written contract. A waitress reported on how she lost her job as soon as she breezily admitted to her employers that she was pregnant. A young man in a Park Royal food warehouse confessed that he had been working non-stop seven days a week since Christmas and with no extra payment for his overtime hours. The mouth of the Community official dropped open in sheer amazement as he listened to the interpreter's translation. "Did he say Park Royal, or Thailand?"

These were the sad front line stories of the bright new workforce from Poland that was supposed to reinvigorate the economy of West London.

Earlier, Community assistant general secretary, Bas Morris, had introduced his officials as they outlined what the trade union Community had to offer Poles. They promised employment security, better wages, safety at work, social benefits, free legal advice, injury compensation. Also freebie rucksacks, pens, chocolate mints and opinions on Arsenal. Community has even introduced a special freephone exclusively for Polish members. Jan Mokrzycki, President of the Federation of Poles in Great Britain, acted both as chair and interpreter as he mopped his brow with exhaustion.

There were some 150 people in the room. More than a third filled out recruitment application forms. The Community officials seemed please; the Poles looked please. Cowboy employers beware! The hard-working tax-paying unionised Polish work force are the children of the Solidarity union which recently overcame communism in Poland and eventually led to the collapse of the Berlin wall. They will be exploited here no longer.

Ealing Gazette February 2nd 2007

The Festive Veterans' Reunions

All the old associations that form the traditional Polish communities of West London seem to wallow in a festive orgy of post-Christmas celebrations that continue from December until Candlemas Day on February 2nd. Many of these once proud organizations now seem to live solely for these annual reunions as they and their friends hug over a shared sacred wafer while wishing each other health and happiness for the coming year. The Polish Centre in Hammersmith (POSK) is the venue for at least 30 of these emotional occasions every season, but there are many more.

Often you find yourself at these events hugging the same people over and over again, each time under the aegis of a different organization. Yet the familiarity and the repetition never seems to pall. Except to their own family, of course.

"Not off for another wafer ceremony, granddad? You went yesterday and the day before."

"Yes Tomek, but that was the artillerymen on Tuesday and the Carpathian Brigade yesterday. Today it's the airmen"

"I thought that was tomorrow?"

"No, it's the Polish Women's Association, tomorrow."

"You on the pull then, granddad?" Embarrassing silence.

"These boring old war veterans," Tomek mutters to my son as they sink back to their "Total War" computer game, while his granddad checks his medals and steps out jauntily to catch the tube to Ravenscourt Park.

Last Sunday, I attended as 80 members of Branch no. 11 of the SPK (Polish ex-Combatants Association), mostly survivors of deportation to Siberia in 1940, reminisced and gossiped over a delicious borsch and cranberry duck. Tearfully they watched 6 little girls, dressed all in white with angelic wings, singing Polish lullaby carols to an imaginary manger.

For the veterans around me the struggle for an independent Poland ended not in 1945 but in 1990. They were proud that they had remained true to their patriotic vision however quaint and unreal that dream had appeared to others. The pre-1939 Poland they fought and yearned for is quite different from modern Poland. It exists still in their collective memory and they bask in its comforting magic surrounded by their veteran friends, discarded song-sheets and empty wine glasses.

Ealing Gazette February 9th 2007

The Eagle has Broadcast

At the top of the steps to the Polish Trade Centre alongside Ealing Broadway station, a photographer was taking individual shots of a group of young hopefuls. I watched a teenager preening in front of the camera, his hat askew at a saucy angle, waistcoat unbuttoned, tartan scarf round his neck. Two blonde girls, looking no older than 17, watched him shyly as they wondered if they had the effrontery to match his postures. It was a photo shoot for the new trainee DJs for "Radio Orla", one of Britain's three Polish radio stations. "Orla" translates as "eagle" - the Polish national symbol.

A corridor to the right leads to the Radio's self-contained premises. They include just 3 rooms: recording studio, waiting room and storage. I glanced through the door of the studio to see the bespectacled features of George Matlock recording a live performance with a couple of eccentric bearded musicians playing Polish Highland music with unashamed gusto. George waved me in the direction of the waiting room.

Here I found 3 young women and one man chatting away as one of them entered Polish news bulletins onto the computer. They were comparing the relative merits of their Polish media studies. They were working in London restaurants or cleaning offices. Their work in the radio, often for many hours several times a week, was unpaid. They needed the work experience as journalists. Also the work was fun and they enjoyed the buzz of having several thousand listeners in England and Ireland.

George managed to free himself and his listeners from the mountain folk. George appears a charming Englishman, but actually both his parents were Polish. His cut-glass English accent contrasts somewhat with his crushed glass Polish diction. An experienced broadcaster, he set up his own station in the spring of 2006 with his own money. All the income is reinvested into improving the facilities. Broadcasts are picked up on the internet 24/7 and are accessible in podcasts. News, music, advice, phone-ins are absorbed by many hard-working homesick Poles in their building sites, kitchens, hospital staff-rooms and lonely flats throughout the land.

Radio Orla seems a labour of requited love.

Ealing Gazette February 16th 2007 –

The Poland Street Gang

We are in the Jazz Cafe, the renovated basement of the Polish Social and Cultural Centre (POSK) in Hammersmith. Low lights, 80's Polish dance music, trendy décor, a long bar serving Polish beer and cocktails. It is the Valentine Dance for the Poland Street Association. Who? The name sounds ominous. No, it is not the name of a Polish street gang.

The chirpy confident well educated young Poles around me, enjoying their knees up, are largely in their twenties. Most appear to have come to London in the last 2 or 3 years. Slowly they have started climbing up the social and economic ladder here. Many work in offices as secretaries, accountants, teachers, journalists, photographers.

Yet the purpose of their new Association was not just to socialize but to campaign for a better deal for their fellow countrymen in this country. During a short break in the music a diminutive young lady with an authoritative voice but a cheeky smile, seized the microphone. It was the Association Secretary, Marzena Cichon, a book designer, who outlined the Association's short but eventful history.

They began as a group who texted each other on the day Pope John Paul II died and were able to organize a commemorative march for their beloved Polish pontiff from Hyde Park to Westminster Cathedral with more than 10,000 participants. They also led a 1000 strong demonstration outside the Polish consulate over the double taxation scandal when Polish authorities were taxing them on their already heavily taxed income in the UK. Each year they lay flowers on the graves of Polish war veterans.

For over a year they have run a free advice centre for young Poles every Saturday at the London Wildlife Centre in Kings Cross. The income from the dance was for this centre. Their earnest new Chairman, Michal Porzyczkowski, employed in a London law firm, stressed on that very day they had had 15 visitors. They needed a larger and better subsidized centre. They have now opened an advice website on the internet and they are planning a specialist advice centre for young Polish mothers.

So far they had largely acted on their own but they were keen to co-operate more closely with the traditional Polish organizations in London. They form a vital bridge linking the old and the new.

February 23rd 2007 – Ealing Gazette

Polish Ambulance Brigade to the Rescue

"Oh no! Not boring Lords Cricket ground again!"

"Oh, don't worry. Not till the summer. There are the FA Cup semi-finals coming up; then there's that concert at the Albert Hall; then the Chelsea Flower Show and afterwards the Trooping of the Colour. We mustn't miss the London Season, you know. Not while we are on duty."

The elite 50-strong London Polish Quadrilateral Division 447Q of the St. John Ambulance, based on the Polish Ealing Community, is getting their seasonal briefing. Watched by Bohdan Mordas, divisional president, and veteran founder of Medical Aid for Poland, Dr. Bozena Laskiewicz, who is the divisional medic, members are diairising the coming events over London as well as some special events in the Polish community.

Adults and young cadets listen attentively to their roster organizer Tom Maramaros. Males are in their white polycotton shirts, black trousers and ties and authoritative black peak caps, while the women volunteers set off their white blouses, black combat duty trousers and yellow bomber jackets with their stylish black hats at a rakish angle.

These are the Polish shock troops of West London. They are ever on call, ready at a moment's notice to cover emergencies or to whisk their elderly and housebound Polish charges to their hospital appointments and social gatherings. They have their shiny ambulance fully equipped with First Aid accessories and the defillibration equipment for heart failures. With efficiency and charm these Polish volunteers, some as young as 9, attend weekly meetings, qualify for their First Aid at Work certificates, raise funds, teach first aid to the public and save lives. They provided the first aid cover during the Queen's Jubilee visit to Ealing and for the Polish President's visit to UK. They have conducted 90,000 hours of voluntary public service for the people of London and given first aid help to 2000 casualties.

It might be a useful initiative for other West London ethnic minority youths to emulate. You feel a true sense of self worth, you share great responsibility with other young people of both sexes and there is always the chance of that free ticket to the first FA cup final in the new Wembley stadium.

Ealing Gazette March 2nd 2007

Who Wants a Separate Polish School?

Aleksandra Podhorodecka peered magisterially over her spectacles at the meeting of Polish teachers and community workers as she called them to order. It was the AGM of the Polish Education Society in Great Britain held in the Polish Centre in Hammersmith.

It had been a stupendous year for Polish children, as she pointed out in her Chairman's report. There were 8 new Polish Saturday schools set up in Britain last year, including one at Shepherd's Bush, to add to the existing 62. More than 800 children had partaken in the Polish language GCSE last summer which was more than double the total of the previous year. So far there were already 1600 applications to sit the exam this year! The examination board was panicking to enlist new examiners in time to do the marking.

In Ealing's primary schools alone the number of Polish speaking children had increased from 205 to 582 over the last 3 years. That was more than 4% of all Ealing's primary school children. The number of Central European high school pupils in Ealing had risen from 224 in 2003 to 403 now. These were remarkable figures and Polish speaking assistants helped those who arrive in school without any knowledge of English. An Ealing Council spokesman had confirmed that "Polish children progress very quickly".

The Polish teachers clucked approvingly at this extraordinary numerical leap in their charges. Suddenly the feathers really began to fly when Dariusz Tereszkowski, a doctor, addressed the meeting over his ambitious plans to set up a Polish language high school in West London within the Government's city academy programme.

He was lambasted by some teachers for trying to keep Polish children segregated from their English peers. This was an unjustified criticism of local schools, they said. Others in turn condemned local "sink" schools and thought Polish children deserved better if it could be provided. All agreed that a professional survey should first evaluate the demand from Polish parents for such a school. In the meantime they preferred to keep the Saturday schools running and send their children to existing local schools.

This will be an explosive issue in the year to come.

Ealing Gazette March 9th 2007

Aimez-vous Polski Jazz?

Did you know that in Communist Poland the question "Lubisz jazz?" ("Do you like jazz?") used to be a highly effective chat up line? What girl could resist that whiff of danger as she sat on a hard floor in a smoked filled room with her boyfriend and listening with studied seriousness to a moody jamming session?

Jazz had been banned in Stalin's day and developed its own underground tradition in Poland quite separate from American blues. It combined folk and classical music resonances to create its own unique sound. It still flourishes in Poland with many bands and jazz clubs as well as devoted radio stations. Its fans in London are now largely middle-aged Poles who have been settling here since the 1960s. They have no venue here in which to listen to Polski Jazz. London has 24 jazz clubs and Ealing has the popular annual Jazz Festival in Walpole Park, but none of these cater for their special brand of music.

Thanks to the Polish Social and Cultural Centre at 238 King Street in Hammersmith this is about to change. On Friday 23rd March the new Jazz Café is about to open. The premises were refurbished following a grant from the Arts Council.

Now we have a cosy area with a long bar, a dance floor, unobtrusive lighting and plenty of nooks and crannies. No hard floors for your bottoms here, just soft red stools. In fact the premises can accommodate 200 jazz devotees comfortably.

The Jazz Café will be offering live Jazz every Saturday evening with performers from Poland as well as from local Home Counties bands. Tickets £10.

On that Friday and Saturday opening visitors will be greeted by one of Poland's leading jazz quartets – Alchemik. They are an eclectic band with a blend of folk and jazz. They will be accompanied by the therapeutic piano work of Janusz Kohut, famous for his jazzed up rendition of Chopin's Revolutionary Etude.

For jazz lovers this is a must. More details: 0208 741 1940. Once you have tasted Polski Jazz you can satisfy your cravings for live music at the Jazz Café every Saturday night.

March 16th 2007 Ealing Gazette

The Polish Jobs Fair

Natwest was quietly confident, Tesco was beaming, Sainsbury's had exceeded all predictions and closed early. Stock Exchange? CBI AGM? Davos seminar? No. None of the above.

It was the 6th British-Polish Recruitment Fair, organized by the British-Polish Chamber of Commerce, sponsored by Western Union and held in Hammersmith Town Hall on March 17th.

Michal Dembinski of BPCC was enthusiastically reeling off statistics. More than 1700 keen young Poles had paid £2 entrance fee to attend. There were 31 organizations with exhibition stalls, manned largely with Polish-speaking staff. These included major employers such as the famous supermarket chains, recruitment agencies such as UK Xchange and internet providers like Londynek.com. Sainsbury's had filled all 300 of their recruitment application forms and left early. Tesco had garnered more than a 100 applications. There were 14 presentation lectures in the adjoining conference room throughout the day. "All the companies here agree," continued Michal, "that recruitment of Poles is far better here than in Poland itself. Everyone here has already jumped the first hurdle. If they are motivated sufficiently to come to England, then they have the right motivation to do the job here."

The lectures included a popular assertiveness workshop. Now Poles, male and female, are not noted for their shyness. But in front of a British employer or interviewer they can dry up.

Also popular was the Write Stuff stall where budding applicants queued for professionally prepared CVs.

I milled around with this army of young hopefuls, brushing against buxom young ladies in canary yellow T-shirts selling lottery tickets for Western Union, and chatting to exhibitors. Everyone agreed it was the best recruitment fair they had attended. "It's very professional," said Alec Smith of the London cab firm, Greyhound Cars, which already employed 30 Polish drivers and now has nearly as many new potential recruits.

As I left this palace of energy and hope I encountered a young man distributing flyers for a Polish waste disposal service to departing exhibitors carting away the contents of their stalls. Meanwhile former visitors were seeking to resell their entrance tickets to new arrivals at half price. The Polish spirit of enterprise is very much alive.

Ealing Gazette March 23rd 2007

The Thoughts of Chairman Jan

Traditionally Polish meetings can be tedious. Adherence to the agenda is chaotic and a Polish speaker will normally use five words where two would suffice. (This will sound familiar to my old colleagues during my days on Ealing Council). When I received notice of the biennial meeting of the Federation of Poles in Great Britain I expected a 5 to 7 hour session. I packed my lunch and my sleeping bag and travelled dejectedly to POSK, the large Polish centre at Hammersmith.

Well, I was wrong. The meeting was chaired very efficiently by Szymon Zaremba, an accountant and former Home Army officer. He challenged long-winded speakers and unnecessary points of order as ruthlessly as he once did the Germans and, to the amazement of delegates, the meeting was over in three hours with all reports debated, a new executive elected, and dinner awaiting us in the Lowiczanka restaurant downstairs still piping hot.

The Federation of Poles is the main representative body of the 600,000 strong Polish community in Great Britain. There were 57 delegates representing 28 major organizations including POSK, the veterans' association (SPK) and the Education Society. The charismatic Federation President, Jan Mokrzycki, a retired dentist, was re-elected. He is a familiar figure to the British media whenever the issue of Polish migrants emerges. His brash no nonsense approach appeals to editors and politicians alike, both in Poland and the UK.

The Federation is not just an association of Polish wrinklies. Organizations representing the new arrivals now join the Federation which runs an information unit for them at its office within the POSK building. It champions the links between the migrants and the trades unions. It publishes a Polish Yellow Pages ("Informator") every 2 years and distributes a popular 80 page handbook on "How to Live and Work in London".

It also organizes an annual Polish festival, the last of which was held in September in Ealing.

So whenever Poles in the UK, young or old, need one voice to speak for them it is the chain-smoking growl of Chairman Jan that provides it.

Ealing Gazette March 30th 2007

A Polish Easter in Ealing

The dominant landmarks in central Ealing are the three iconic 19th century spires which lift my heart every time I espy them from a distance. Ealing Town Hall, Christ Church and the Polish Church seem a natural manifestation of the god-fearing confident municipal pride of the old Queen of the Suburbs.

I love the Polish Church. Consecrated in 1986 as the Church of the Blessed Virgin Mary Mother of the Church, this former Methodist church was acquired by the largest Polish parish in the UK. This Catholic community has actually flourished in Ealing since 1948.

Within those whitewashed walls more than 4500 Poles worship mass every Sunday, spread across 8 services from 8.30 am till 10.30 at night. Shoppers in Ealing Broadway are often astonished to see whole families kneeling and praying outside the church walls, rain or shine, as the building is filled to overcapacity.

Commenting on the numbers, parish priest, Father Krzysztof Wojcieszak, explains that "last year the church witnessed 172 christenings, 83 children taking their first Holy Communion and celebrated 209 weddings." (There were also 48 funerals. Can you spot the demographic trend here?)

During Easter week the number of worshippers increases. On Palm Sunday the congregation display their palm leaves distributed by eager young girl guides, and listen attentively to Jesus' suffering and execution as they follow the white bas-relief carvings around the church depicting each agonizing Station of the Cross.

On Thursday the mass commemorates the last supper and on Good Friday the church plunges into darkness for the all night vigil by the tomb.

Then throughout Easter Saturday families pour in clutching their baskets of painted eggs, salt, bread, sausages and a lamb sculptured in sugar. Easter egg decorating (not the chocolate variety!) is a traditional Polish folk art, which children display on this day and scrutinize each other's offerings competitively. Then they squeal in delight as they dodge the holy water sprinkled by the priest on food and families alike.

The families disperse to consume their blessed nourishment for Easter Sunday lunch. But first they repair back to their church, now resplendent in white light and white flowers, to celebrate the triumphant resurrection of the Lord.

For Easter service details please ring 0208 567 1746

Ealing Gazette April 6th 2007

A Barbaric Ritual

Were you perhaps woken on Easter Monday morning by the sound of young women screaming?

If so, I hope you were not too alarmed. No need to activate your local Neighbourhood Watch. In fact you were probably witnessing the enactment of the primeval Polish tradition of "dyngus". It falls regularly on Easter Monday and it consists of Poles, male and female, soaking each other with water. It signifies the washing away of sin and it is a spring fertility rite. I suppose it is only fair that after the piety of Holy Week, Poles tend to let their (soaking wet) hair down somewhat.

I was drawn into this pleasantly barbaric ritual when I visited friends at Green Avenue in Northfields early that fateful morning. I was assailed by water pistols and ended up being dunked during a watery dog fight with plastic bottles in their back garden. Then after a reassuring glass of wine, I joined forces with this family and we proceeded, four strong and armed with water propellants and water-bombs, towards another Polish house in nearby Haslemere Avenue. Local residents watched with trepidation at their garden gates as we proceeded menacingly like a modern aquatic equivalent of Doc Holliday and the Earp brothers on their way to their Slavonic OK Corral.

At the second destination, all hell broke loose. The female household defended their property with great resolve and screamed for England every time they were drenched. The very youngest called in her young English neighbours armed with pump action water guns, while further Polish families descended onto this battlefield site. The skirmishes covered the street outside as well as the garden and the crucial last stand enveloped the tap in the rear garden as both sides battled for this energy source to replenish their buckets, pistols and plastic canisters while trying to dodge the water bombs raining down on them from the second floor.

Eventually everyone settled down, changed into dry clothes and sipped their mulled honey wine while the children were rewarded with chocolate eggs. A female latecomer turned up at 3 o'clock with a water container and attacked the resting veterans upon which the newly soaked males unceremoniously picked her up and chucked her into a bath full of cold water on the first floor. Honour was satisfied.

At least this year there was no police intervention. Some years ago my friends and I were ordered by a policeman to desist as "Water is a dangerous weapon." I could not agree more.

Ealing Gazette April 13th 2007

Kasia's Polish kitchens

"The Oaks" shopping precinct off Acton High Street, with its new pound-stretcher shops and economically priced supermarkets, may not be your Burlington Arcade resplendent with decadence and luxury. But it is a pleasant, airy and clean walkway filled with some of Acton's less affluent shoppers consisting mainly of young families or the elderly with their eye for a bargain or cheap frozen food.

After a successful shopping expedition in this covered precinct, where better to rest your weary bones, chill out and chat with your friends than Kasia's Café? White clean floors and wide aisles for prams and wheelchairs beckon the weary shopper inside, while prim and polite young Polish waitresses can serve you delicious home-made meals, salads and cakes. It is an ideal stopping place before the heavily laden shoppers trot off home with their purchases or take the lift upstairs to the car park.

Although the most common meals available in Kasia's are the cheap and nourishing English breakfasts which are served all day, their real speciality is Polish food. Serving the traditional lip-smacking dumplings (pierogi) with a wide variety of fillings, stuffed cabbage and bigos (the hunter's rich meat and sauerkraut stew), all priced in the region of £3.50, it is possibly the cheapest unsubsidized venue for a hot Polish meal in the Borough.

So who is Kasia? I met her one Saturday morning. Her name is Katarzyna (Kasia) Richards and she comes from an artistic Polish family. She moved to London in 1968, worked as an illustrator for medical handbooks, and has been married for over 30 years to an English insurance executive. Following some shrewd property investments the retired couple wanted to help her impoverished countrymen by offering legal registered employment to Polish cooks and waitresses and by serving good inexpensive Polish food.

The first Kasia's Café opened in 2005. It's a small cosy eating place in Acton High Street near the West London Trades Union Club.

Kasia's new larger premises in "The Oaks" opened last year. "We have no smoking, no alcohol, good security from the arcade staff and a European cuisine with everything prepared freshly on the premises," says Kasia. "All ages, all religions, all nationalities eat here. It's a delightful and safe place for all families to try their first Polish meal." So if you want to partake in the trendy new Polish life-style in West London but you are financially somewhat prudent, Kasia's is a good place to start.

Ealing Gazette April 20th 2007

Football Comes to Poland

The news hit the Polish West London internet chatter market at around midday the previous Wednesday. Yes, it was true! UEFA had awarded the right to stage its European Champions Tournament in 2012 jointly to Poland and Ukraine.

When I first heard this I was dumbstruck. Poland and Ukraine were the outsiders. Italians with their beautiful stadiums, classy motorways, world class footballers and sunny beaches were sworn favourites. Sure, they may have blotted their copybook somewhat with a few fixed match results and their baton-wielding police had practised karate chops with their truncheons on discontented Manchester United fans. But this was the land of vendettas, where things occasionally get a little corrupt and violent between the shrugged shoulders and the romantic songs about Sorrento.

Suddenly the shrugging and the "cantare" had to stop. It was the 83 million strong Polish-Ukrainian conglomerate which had won the day on the first round of voting. UEFA had turned east to two of those countries which had been pressing their eager faces to the glass as they watched the Western football megastars strut their stuff in the past. Now my fellow London Poles had to take in the fact that the baton had certainly passed to our two nations.

After the initial euphoria came the nightmare doubts. Were our stadiums too old? What about Polish and Ukrainian roads? What about the head-banging fans? Are the police up to scratch? Never mind, we thought, we have 5 years to get it right.

We dreaded though what the British papers might say. Strangely they said almost nothing. It was not even mentioned on the morning TV news summaries. We could stand being praised. We could stand being vilified. We could not stand being ignored. Did the British really not care?

Then I turned to the BBC news website. I searched for commentaries on the main news bulletin. 356 comments! That's more like it! Some compared us to the Third World. Some said this was a great step forward for UEFA. Most criticism was reserved for Italy anyway. The majority seemed to be rubbing their hands with glee. Many British fans were looking forward to "cheap vodka, cheap beer, and beautiful women." Well, somebody has the right priorities!

April 27th 2007 Ealing Gazette

Beneath the Black Obelisk

"Katyn" – (pronounced "cut-teen") was the name whispered mysteriously by adults in Communist Poland when the children were supposedly not listening. It was the unmentionable word. A child could be expelled from school for repeating it in front of its classmates. In a country which displayed the evils of the German occupation at every turn, this secret word suggested something more sinister even than Auschwitz.

Of course the free Poles in UK were determined to bear witness to this awful crime after 4200 Polish officers were found murdered in the Katyn Forest in 1943. In 1976 they had erected a huge black obelisk in Gunnersbury Cemetery near the Chiswick roundabout. In defiance of the then British government, to whom "Katyn" was also a taboo word, the Royal Borough of Kensington & Chelsea had given the Poles planning permission for this sombre monument as long as the name of the perpetrators was not displayed. So only the date of the massacre was shown - "1940". In the circumstances the date said it all.

Unlike those who perished in the German death camps or during the Warsaw Uprising, these war victims, and some 10,000 other Polish officers, policemen and farmers who had been shot by the Soviet NKVD in other parts of Russia, were never commemorated and the criminals never punished. The Nazi invaders who found the Katyn graves in 1943 accused Stalin of committing this crime in 1940; Stalin promptly said the Germans killed them in 1941 when they invaded Russia. The Western Allies believed the Soviet version right up until 1992 when the Russian Government admitted the crime and revealed the sites of the other massacres. The Poles who knew the truth had been vilified as warmongers. The prolonged denial of the crime had intensified the poison surrounding it.

"Not all wounds heal with time," said a tall elegant elderly gentleman with a white moustache, as he addressed a silent crowd of wreath-bearers in front of the obelisk last Sunday. "Some leave deep scars." It was Ryszard Kaczorowski, the last Polish President in exile, reminding Poles, both young and old, how this crime had cut so deep into the Polish psyche.

The Polish Ambassador, Mrs Barbara Tuge-Erecinska, urged that truth about such crimes must be revealed. “Otherwise”, she stated, “others feel they can perform similar crimes with impunity”.

Wise words for what also happened to be the fourth anniversary of the continuing genocide in Darfur.

Ealing Gazette May 4th 2007

The Battle of the Banks

As I was passing the HSBC branch at Ealing Broadway, my eye lighted on a Polish poster in the window. "Welcome to the Polish branch of our bank," it said. "Multicultural banking."

I wondered. Was this part of the quest for that mythical beast – the "Polish Pound"? This was not a reference to Stephan Pound, our ebullient Ealing North MP, who occasionally makes speeches in Polish. No, it was a phenomenon I had read about recently in the "Financial Times" (Don't sneer. The FT is an excellent cure for insomnia.). Apparently the spending power of an average Polish migrant in Britain comes to more than £6000 a year after tax and rent. That amounts to an input of £4 billion a year into the UK economy.

The banks wanted a slice of the action. The HSBC was first off the mark last year, printing leaflets in Polish and recruiting Polish-speaking staff. Polish migrants were offered so-called Passport Accounts with cheap money transfers to Poland and debit cards. This was great news for Poles who were mostly unfamiliar with cheque books. Poles had leaped 15 years ago from a cash economy directly to a credit card economy. Also no need now for all the earlier hassle of presenting rent books, utility bills and passports to open an account. Just an I.D. card was enough.

Natwest followed in January with Welcome Accounts which included money transfer accounts to Poland. This April, Lloyds TSB announced a new Silver Account which gave Poles a second debit card to be sent to relatives to draw money from a TSB account in Poland. Rival financial institutions vie for Polish business with glossy ads in the free Polish press.

Now this poster was telling me that HSBC had a new initiative – a Polish Business Unit. The Ealing HSBC Polish Unit Manager, Monika Merritt, explained that the Ealing Centre offers Poles commercial advice and investment in Polish. They assess business plans, offer equipment finance, advise on pension funds. "We are a bank, not a pawnbroker," she said, but she is pleased how many Polish businesses, including delicatessens, construction companies, accountants and translators, have proved to be sound investments. Similar HSBC Polish Centres have opened in Greenford, Acton, Hammersmith and Kensington.

The battle for the "Polish Pound" is stepping up.

Ealing Gazette May 11th 2007

The Upper Room Project

There were at least 100 people in the room sitting eating quietly at long wooden tables. They appeared to be mostly middle aged men of all races with weathered features, often ruddy-faced and bewhiskered. Some were actually much younger than they looked. The few women had faces ravaged by their gruelling existence.

The portions looked big as they hungrily lapped up the sauce on their food with pieces of buttered bread. A queue of stragglers had just finished collecting their food from the serving hatch behind which stood a formidable array of ladies whose racial origin reflected the various ethnic origins of the diners.

The room was well furnished with books and magazines in English and other languages, especially Polish.

I was in the famous Upper Room at St Saviour's Church in Cobbold Road, off Askew Road.

Project Manager Bruce Marquart explained that the daily meal provided to all who came was initiated 16 years ago by a network of volunteers from 45 churches and Christian charities around West London. 6 part-time staff and 3 volunteers worked each day providing 90 meals, laundry facilities and advice, as well as moral sustenance. The centre offered training facilities for lower skilled jobs and a website for job seekers in UK. In the last month alone some 40 clients, mostly Poles, had qualified for the CSCS card and were able to get qualified construction jobs near Manchester. A similar programme was being prepared for a Europe-wide job placement facility.

Former Polish nurse Halina Jakubik, who first came to the centre last year after losing her job and now works part-time in the kitchen, told me

"This place put me back on my feet. I have some money again and can help my family in Poland. Now I can requalify as a nurse in England."

She confirmed that about 60% of those attending were Poles down on their luck. I chatted to them. Some had no jobs; some worked nights as security; many were squatters or lived in parks; others just needed a good square meal. One had been woken up and robbed by a gang in Acton Park that very morning. All were grateful for this facility and the opportunity for work and professional advice in Polish that it gave them.

Ominously, none could see themselves returning to Poland yet. That would mean a total loss of face; after all they had been writing to their families telling them how well they were faring here.

Ealing Gazette May 18th 2007

Democracy behind the Bunker

An anonymous Hammersmith Councillor (he had better remain anonymous!) once told me that the black and grey façade of POSK, the Polish Social and Cultural Centre, was the ugliest building on King Street. Piffle! What about the tall Premier Travel Inn directly opposite? And neither of them could compete in ugliness with the now doomed Hammersmith Town Hall Annexe!

Ugliness, like beauty, is in the eye of the beholder. To London Poles, POSK is a palace of culture. Here octogenarian émigré elites rub shoulders with the smug nouveau riche and the toiling young masses. Within its welcoming walls is the largest Polish library outside Poland with its priceless historical archives to which Polish and British historians make regular pilgrimages. In the 1960s, at the height of the Cold War, Polish pensioners sacrificed their last savings to erect this fortress to nourish the spirit of a free Poland and protect their precious library which an insensitive British government (yes, them!) was trying to disband. Books were transferred here in columns of private cars from Kensington over a period of many months.

Not a bookworm? You can watch a children's play or a cabaret in the large theatre, enjoy the changing art exhibits behind the foyer, hang out in the plush newly opened jazz café or enjoy the delights of Polish cooking in the legendary "Lowiczanka" where war-time generals once consumed their borsch and drowned their smoked herring in vodka. There is the Pilsudski Institute with its sepia photos and memorabilia from pre-war Poland, the sedate Conrad Society, a club and bridge room with a terrace view from top, a ground floor café and bookshop, lecture halls for the Polish University Abroad and offices for many Polish organizations.

Despite its external bunker image POSK has always been a democratic institution with several thousand members and an annual turnover exceeding £2 million. During a 5 hour slog of an AGM last week, 13 members of the Executive (no sleeping members here!) described their activities over the previous year.

UK born Chairman Olgierd Lalko, square-shouldered and square-jawed, exuded confidence and common sense as he weighed the balance between commercial astuteness and the rich social agenda required by POSK's charity status. With shoulders like that we know he can carry forward the historic burden to a promising future.

Ealing Gazette May 25th 2007

Beer Cans in Greenford

The Recreation Ground between Oldfield Lane North and Greenford Road is a pretty featureless area of grassland. No ducks to feed or trees to admire. Yet it has a popular children's playground, many benches and plenty space for budding footballers and skateboarders.

As I crossed it one hot day, I saw two of the benches occupied by some young Polish skinheads. They were chatting amiably, soaking in the spring sunshine and holding cans of Zywiec beer. They were listening to a football match on a portable radio. For reasons not very clear to me other park users seemed to be avoiding them. However I joined them to listen to the match.

As we chatted I pointed out that drinking alcohol there is likely to become a criminal offence from July onwards. Notice of a proposed restriction order on drinking in public in Greenford Green and Perivale was being advertised by Ealing Council in their monthly magazine. If police were to catch them with an open can their drink would be confiscated and they could be fined up to £500.

Their jaws dropped. On a scale of 1 to10 their knowledge of English was below zero. They were not illegal migrants. They worked hard as kitchen porters, as cleaners, as builders' mates. They sent money to their parents. They paid national insurance and were registered to work. They were even on the electoral register. But just then they did not feel very enfranchised.

"So where are we supposed to drink? How are we expected to relax? Where do we go?" they asked. They live in crowded multi-occupational homes, 2 to 3 in a room, often "hot bedding", i.e. sharing beds which they occupied in shifts.

I sympathized with their plight though I pointed out that some late night drinkers were a real nuisance and very intimidating to local residents, especially for those with young families. However it is true that there is nowhere for young Poles to meet socially in Greenford.

At least on Sundays they now have a local mass to attend at Our Lady of Visitation Church on Greenford Road, away from the huddled masses of the Polish church in Ealing Broadway. Like most of his flock, the new young mission priest, Father Janusz Gorczyca, does not yet have a permanent residence. The Greenford Poles still have a long way to go.

Ealing Gazette 1st June 2007

What's in a Name?

You must have heard the story of the Pole who went to see the optician.

The optician points to the traditional board with the usual jumble of letters such as K, Z and so on.

"Now," says the optician, "can you recognize anything on that board?"

"Recognize anything?" says the surprised Pole. "Of course I can recognize him. It's my cousin!"

Growing up in West London in the 1950s, when Poles seemed to form the only ethnic minority around, our one characteristic that distinguished our white skins from our fellow white-skinned English pupils at school was our strange tongue-twisting surnames. They seemed a burden sometimes, especially in secondary schools, where we all still addressed each other by our surnames. ("You did what!?" asks my son disdainfully.)

A teacher would read out the register of names and then deliberately mangle the Polish surname for a cheap laugh. My regular nickname at school was Mousehole or Moses, and both were given me by a mean Latin teacher. He labelled my friend Kaczmarek - "Catsmeat" and Przedrzymirski as simply "Swish". Nice!

Cue the playground bully chanting your nickname "Lead us, Moses. Where's your rod?"

"Why don't you change your name to something simpler?" asked another teacher, "Like Smith, for instance?"

Simpler? Well my parents were never able to pronounce a name like Smith anyway, with that characteristic tongue-in-the-teeth "th" sound, so unique to English.

Now questions like that would be considered politically incorrect, of course.

Ultimately our names ceased to be the Mark of Cain and became a badge of distinction which made us stand out in a crowd.

In fact, even now, despite all the other ethnic minorities that inhabit London, our surnames still seem to be among the longest and most difficult to pronounce. And we are proud of them. Only Tamil surnames seem to be longer.

And in case you ask, a "-ski" at the end of a Polish (or Russian) surname denotes the preposition "of", like the French "de" and the German "von"; while an "-icz" ending means "son of".

Oh yes! And a female "-ski" becomes a "-ska", so if you are chatting up a Mrs Kowalska (the Polish equivalent of Smith) remember to revert to a "-ski" ending when you meet her husband!

Ealing Gazette June 8th 2007

The Year of the General

Just mention the word "General" on its own to elderly London Poles and it can only mean one person. General Wladyslaw Anders. A hero to his soldiers, his was a household name to many British people as well.

On Friday June 15th the POSK centre in Hammersmith is hosting a conference, organized by the Polish University Abroad, with 11 lectures in English, to commemorate the General's life and achievements. It will be followed by a further session in Polish on Saturday with children encouraged to join in the discussion.

It is difficult to exaggerate the popular appeal of this charismatic soldier, who was plucked out of a Soviet jail in 1941 and placed at the head of an army of bewildered starving frost-bitten Poles amnestied from Siberian labour camps. In 1939 the Soviets had deported more than one and a half million Polish civilians while 20,000 officers and policemen were shot. Anders miraculously survived.

Like Moses before Pharaoh, he succeeded eventually in persuading a sceptical Stalin to allow not only his ragged Polish army, but also thousands of malnourished Polish women and children, to leave Russia. Under British protection, he created a Polish military and civilian enclave in Persia and Iraq with schools, libraries, sports clubs and hospitals, while bringing his army of exiles up to strength.

Then he led his devoted men to fight the Germans in the Italian campaign, leading them to victory at Monte Cassino. His army also liberated Ancona and Bologna.

Deprived of his Polish citizenship after the war by the Communists, Anders remained in exile in London. He was the foremost champion of the Free Poles. A former Olympic horse rider, an excellent dancer and bridge player, he cut quite a dash with the ladies. After his death in 1970 he was buried with his fallen soldiers on the slopes of Cassino, some 900 miles from his homeland. His widow, a former singer and Polish soldiers' sweetheart, will be present at the inauguration of the conference on Friday and Londoners are invited to attend.

The General remained a figure of hatred and scorn with the Communists regime in Poland until 1989. Now the Polish Senate has officially declared 2007 as the Year of General Anders. Streets have been renamed after him in every city in Poland. A grateful nation is ready to honour him at last.

Ealing Gazette June 15th 2007

The Film-Maker of Shaa Road

I always enjoyed attending receptions at one of the houses in a leafy Acton avenue called Shaa Road. The hostess of these cultural events always thought it a strange name for a street but it was named, I believe, after a prosperous Mayor of London from Tudor times.

This hostess was a plucky and energetic Polish lady called Jagna Wright, a former Warsaw journalist, who had married her husband Stephen in 1977 and settled in Acton some 20 years ago.

Like everyone brought up in Communist Poland she was imbued with a deep awareness of the genocide and destruction that Poland suffered under Nazi occupation. It was only after living here that she became aware of the extent of another terrible reality of the Second World War. She met elderly Polish émigrés, including her own aunt, who had witnessed and survived the massacres and destruction wrought on the Polish population by the Soviets. She believed their story had to be told.

In 2001 she joined up with a professional film editor from North Ealing, Aneta Naszynska, to make a documentary at which these living survivors (who included my mother) were able at last to bear witness to their sufferings. Almost all had been mere children during the mass deportations and their observations were therefore all the more acute. Devoid of any heroics these survivors recounted how their families perished from cold, hunger and disease in the Soviet outlands. Of the 1.7 million deported, barely 110,000 were evacuated 2 years later to Iran.

Jagna called her film "The Forgotten Odyssey". It was a race with time to ensure that her subjects lived long enough to record their testimony. Within a few years many of them had indeed died.

Jagna was relentless in her efforts to have the film screened publicly in Britain. It made the History Channel. In the United States, she awoke the sleeping giant of a second generation of Polish-Americans anxious to learn more of the wartime fate of their parents.

She and Aneta then set themselves the ambitious task of filming a second documentary, "The Other Truth", a 3 hour trilogy about Polish-Jewish relations.

Sadly, last Saturday, Jagna lost her own race with time as the cancer she had struggled with for five years finally caught up with her. She was only 57 and her friends are distraught. There will be a private funeral for her husband, 3 children and close friends but her public achievements will be commemorated in due course.

Ealing Gazette June 29th 2007

Towards A Sad Second Anniversary

We are approaching the second anniversary of the London bombings on July 7th. It is a time for sad reflection for every Londoner, and unfortunately also for renewed vigilance.

Nothing underlines the close integration of young Poles into the daily fabric of the London scene more starkly than the fact the largest number of victims of foreign nationality who died on that dreadful day were Polish.

Three young Polish women, unknown to each other, all perished on the Piccadilly Line between Kings Cross and Russell Square.

Nearest to her destination at the time of the explosion was 29 year old Karolina Gluck who worked as a college receptionist. She was every inch a Londoner. She had a black fiancé, wore a metal St George Cross in her belly button and her friends called her "Sunshine" because of her sunny disposition.

Younger still was 23 year old pretty Monika Suchocka, an economics graduate and trainee accountant, who lived in a cramped flat with 2 friends in North London. She loved to sing and had found the time during her 2 month stay in London to join a choir.

Anna Brandt was 41 and she was on her way to Hammersmith where she worked as a cleaner. One of her two grown-up daughters had just arrived in London and she was looking forward to meeting her. Anna had ambitions too. She aimed to earn enough money to bring over her husband and start up a restaurant business in West London.

These were not the only losses that the Polish community suffered on July 7th. One of the victims on the bombed No. 30 bus in Tavistock Square was Giles Hart, a former Chairman of the Polish Solidarity Campaign. He was married to a Polish wife who was the head of a Polish Saturday school in East London. He was posthumously awarded a Knights Cross of Merit by the Polish President.

Giles had been no stranger to Hammersmith as many of the campaign meetings he chaired took place in POSK on King Street where he also founded the Polish Refugees Rights Group. There is a proposal to erect a plaque in his honour in Ravenscourt Park next year.

Aspiring young Poles continue to live, work (and die) unseen and unheard amongst us fellow Londoners.

Ealing Gazette July 6th 2007

Trying Out for Polish Big Brother

As you cross Hammersmith Flyover towards London you can see the massive edifice of Hotel Novotel on your left.

The previous week this luxury 4 star hotel witnessed the latest recruitment drive for Poles in London. It was not a job fair but at least 70 hopefuls saw this as a significant career move. Endemol Polska had come to London seeking suitable volunteers for the next Polish Big Brother show in September.

It was a mixed crowd of ego-tripping star-obsessed Poles who had turned up for this emotional treadmill. As the aspiring candidates lined up in front of the registration desk you could see the usual array of diffident short cropped young men and chatty young brunettes and blondes (some of them even natural blondes), interspersed with a few middle aged entrants.

The main initiator of the programme, Jaroslaw Ostaszkiewicz, explained to journalists that he was keen to recruit two or three participants who lived and worked in the UK.

"We think," he told us, "that a person who has chosen to find work abroad must have courage, be able to adapt to new circumstances and have a detached view of his own countrymen because of the experience of living in the West." He did not rule out casting Polish-speaking foreigners, perhaps even a non-white.

Many of the applicants had been in the West for several years. This was obvious from their use of English household equivalents for a number of Polish words. They appeared suitably shameless. Many admitted to cheating on their partners and were ready to strip off in public. The organizers were rubbing their hands with glee. More than 60 of them passed their first audition.

Some came for the money and others for the fame. They included university graduates working as cleaners who were desperate to improve their social status. Others were already successful but seeking a change, such as the company director who flew over from California and designed palaces for the super rich.

My favourite was a 58 year woman accountant out to have a good time who admitted to snoring heavily. She thought her snoring would drive the others to sleep in the lounge leaving her alone in the bedroom. Other participants beware!

Ealing Gazette July 13th 2007

The Gazette's Polish Sister

There I was, as usual, last Friday morning at my local newsagents near Ealing Common station buying my favourite newspaper. The local Gazette gives me the sensational news stories occurring in West London. However I also want to remind myself what I had written the previous week for my column, as by Friday my activities of the past week seem enveloped in the mists of oblivion.

Suddenly on the shelf next to my reserved Gazette I espied a similar newspaper with the same layout and lead story but beneath a red banner which read "Gazeta Polska". (For the benefit of you non-Polish muggles that means "Polish Newspaper ").

Gingerly I picked up this newspaper and found that it reflected news story after story of the usual Ealing events but written in Polish. I bought the newspaper and continued to compare both papers.

In fact the first 7 pages of the Polish version were straight translations from selected stories in the Ealing & Acton Gazette and next two were articles about the latest events in Poland. I was shocked to see my own bewhiskered features also appear over my humble little column in a Polish translation. Afterwards, the remaining texts were in English and identical to the main English version.

I was surprised and cheered by the sheer boldness of this experiment, probably the first of its kind for any local London paper. The editors of the Gazette and of the venerable Polish Daily (which had been published every day in West London since 1941) had agreed to provide a joint information service for the burgeoning Polish population in Ealing and Acton which would keep those with language difficulties aware of what was happening in the area and give them a chance to practice their English.

It was a salute to the fact that Ealing Borough has the largest concentration of Poles in the UK and they are all residents, consumers, transport users and council tax payers who contribute richly to the life of the borough as well benefit from its services.

I have a hunch this experiment may be copied elsewhere, perhaps also in other languages. Well done, Gazette! Well done, Polish Daily!

Ealing Gazette July 20th 2007

A Polish Teller of Tales

So have all you Potter aficionados, young and old, finished reading the 607 pages of the last book yet? Do you hanker to visit a real castle now with hidden chambers accessible only to those with the right password? Then I suggest you make your away to the meandering corridors of the Polish Hogwarts (the POSK building) on King Street in Hammersmith.

One of the most difficult places to find (be very very nice to the receptionist) is the elegant Joseph Conrad room. If you are permitted to enter this hallowed sanctuary you come across a magnificent table, surrounded by dark book-filled cabinets interspersed with narrow passages of which only one leads to a further hidden chamber. This is the nerve-centre of the Joseph Conrad Society (UK) which exists to honour and promote the works of a prolific nineteenth century writer and seaman called Joseph Conrad.

The year 2007 is actually the 150th anniversary of Conrad's birth. The Society has prepared a rich international programme commemorating the works of this deeply moral author of adventure stories. His books are full of anti-heroes struggling against the weakness of their own characters. Many reflect the author's experience of the treacherous seas and the corruption of colonial life. Novels like "Lord Jim" and "Nostromo" have been filmed. More famous was Coppola's "Apocalypse Now", based on Conrad's "Heart of Darkness". It shows the depths of an evil far more sinister than Lord Voldemort. Ominously Conrad's novel "The Secret Agent", written in 1907, predicted how terrorists would try to blow up London and gave Hitchcock the plot-line for his film "Sabotage".

Conrad wrote his magnificent stories in English, but he was actually Polish. His parents were deported to Siberia by the Russians. He only learned to speak and write in English in his late twenties. Like many later Polish émigrés he had excessively impeccable manners, a wispy beard, a horrid English accent and a name - Jozef Teodor Konrad Korzeniowski – that was too much of a tongue-twister for the British reading public (are you surprised?). He was offered a knighthood but was too proud to accept. And anyway, why make your name even longer?

His romantic Polish soul led him into a number of frustrating failed love affairs, but he also kept to the Polish practice of kissing the hand of any lady that he met. He once kissed the hand of a maid and she fled in terror to the police. That and his failed love affairs may have led to his famous saying:- "Being a woman is a terribly difficult task, since it consists principally in dealing with men."

Ealing Gazette July 27th 2007

Red Ken is in the Building

The Polish Centre staff in Hammersmith was anxiously awaiting the arrival of their VIP guest. The executive members had gathered excitedly in the entrance hall. The cream cakes were ready in the Jazz Café basement.

As Chairman Olgierd Lalko issued another round of instructions a quiet unassuming figure slipped into the building from the direction of Ravenscourt Park station, dressed in a light suit and unceremoniously sporting a shoulder bag. It took a couple of minutes for the welcoming committee to notice him. A beaming Ken Livingstone had arrived.

The reception committee swarmed around him like bees but the Mayor was his usual diffident self as he shook the hand of committee members and staff alike. He posed for photos with everyone in his path.

The Chairman whisked him on a whirlwind tour of the ground floor gallery, the Conrad room, the library and the theatre. As they briefed him on the wonders of POSK's extraordinary rise from the ashes, Red Ken carried on his charm offensive. He watched an opera rehearsal in the theatre. Then he was guided into the permanent exhibition in the Eagle Chamber. He was tickled pink at the sight of pre-war Polish bus tickets ("So you had oyster cards in Warsaw in 1939?") and a ticket to the previous London Olympics, held in 1948, and priced at 7/6d.

A crowded Jazz Café awaited him, as well as the cream cakes. He dealt with the cakes first and the Polish audience after when he told them they were all Londoners now and should hold a celebratory Polish festival in Trafalgar Square.

The Mayor dealt promptly with the questions. Boris Johnson? He recommended his opponent's "scary" new book and suggested they have a "High Noon" confrontation in POSK. Polish Saturday schools? Great idea as it kept children off the streets and kept them close to their parents' culture. Freedom pass for over 60s? It would stay.

Cameras flashed, journalists' mikes protruded invitingly and the Livingstone cavalcade pushed slowly through the milling scrum towards the exit.

"He left us feeling like we were one big family," said POSK volunteer guide Monika Skowronska. "There was a sense of electricity and buzz in the building on a scale that I had never seen there before."

Ealing Gazette August 3rd 2007

Save St Andrews Church

I watched them in wonder sauntering piously towards the communion rail. As the bright sunlight poured in from up high through the battle scenes embedded in the stained glass windows, I could discern hues of brilliant gold reflecting the sands of Tobruk, and deep dark green mixed with bright red from the red poppies on the green Cassino mountain slopes, as they etched themselves onto the white summer clothing of the worshippers below.

These bright garish windows of the St Andrew Bobola church in Hammersmith commemorate the tank crews, pilots, paratroopers and other branches of the Polish armed forces in the Second World War.

Above the altarpiece a large glass roundel depicting a winged white Holy Ghost surmounts a gigantic sad crucifix. Yet these windows give the church an uplifting celebratory effect which is not in conflict with the deep vibes emanating from the historic memorial stones dedicated to Polish heroes and martyrs.

A side chapel also houses the holy painted icon of Our Lady of Kozhelsk, carved by a prisoner in the Russian monastery from which several thousand Polish officers had been carted to their execution in the Katyn Forest.

The squat white tower of this remarkable church is visible over Ravenscourt Park. The church is accessible from Goldhawk Road at the Paddenswick Road roundabout and is part of the Polish heritage tour organized by Hammersmith Council.

For the traditional Polish congregation however this is the "garrison" church. Within its walls are echoes of Poland's tragic and troubled past but a large proportion of those who attend the four masses held every Sunday, and who contribute to the cultural life and social services of the parish, are young families who do not feel so burdened by the shadows of its past.

Last year this historic edifice was faced with a massive renovation project. The total cost exceeded £660,000 and a bank loan had to be raised. Up went the scaffolding. Up too went the generous contributions from young and old.

Last Sunday the scaffolding was down. The parish priest, Father Bronislaw Gostomski, was finally able to announce from the pulpit that the work on the church was finished. London Poles had contributed £185,000 so far.

Debts still remain but this historic gem has been saved for posterity.

Ealing Gazette August 10th 2007

Honouring Soldiers' Day

During its Golden Age in the XVIth century, Poland-Lithuania was the largest state in Europe and saw itself as the replica of the old Roman Republic – a haven of peace and prosperity, religiously tolerant, democratic and yet devout. Later, when its vast territories were overrun by despotic invaders and Poland ceased to exist as an independent state, a rich messianic cocktail of honour, song, beauty, pain, sacrifice, death and the Virgin Mary became the hallmark of Poland's survival. After each failed insurrection this heady romantic mixture and the resulting bloodshed were mocked by the next young generation and then inherited wholesale in turn by their children.

In 1920 the cynics and romantics united when their new state was threatened by a Soviet Russian invasion intent on submerging all of war-weary Europe in a Bolshevik revolution. The Red Army was defeated at the very gates of Warsaw. Devout Poles called this event the "Miracle on the Vistula".

The battle date was August 15th. This happened to be the Feast of the Assumption of the Virgin Mary, whom Poles had crowned Queen of Poland more than 200 years before. So August 15th officially became Soldiers' Day, as well as a religious feast day.

This week the Polish Ex Combatants Association commemorated Soldiers' Day with a special mass for those who died for their country in past centuries, including the recent deaths of Polish soldiers in Iraq and Afghanistan.

There followed a concert in the Polish Centre in Hammersmith. The tremulous voices of a mixed school choir of 18 year olds from Western Poland emotionally massaged the old veterans and their stern standard bearers with resonant battle hymns and unashamedly romantic patriotic songs that brought to mind the medieval wars with the Teutonic Knights, the defeat of the Turks at Vienna, the Napoleonic wars, the later failed insurrections, Monte Cassino and the hopeless Warsaw Uprising of 1944 where more than 200,000 perished, and, finally, the bloodless triumph of Solidarity.

Grateful veterans gave the youngsters a standing ovation. Many young Poles are indeed proud of these veterans; others find this burden of death and remembrance oppressive and opt for a prosperous career bereft of Poland's weighty past.

"OK. Let them prosper," a veteran paratrooper told me, "then we in turn can be proud of them!"

Ealing Gazette – August 24th 2007

A Factory of Bridal Dreams

When archaeologists in Xian first discovered the tomb with the forest of Chinese terracotta soldiers, their sense of wonder reflected mine as I walked through the front door of The Bridal Gallery in South Ealing Road and negotiated my way around an orchard of mannequins dressed in the most sumptuous wedding dresses I had ever seen.

Beyond this barrier, a smiling Agata Czarnota guided me to a white sofa and a bracing cup of morning coffee, as she explained the history of the shop which she has owned now for 3 years.

Though most of her clients are Polish, she serves all nationalities and has organized weddings for Kurds (apparently their wedding colour is green), Irish and Nigerians as well as other ethnic groups. "The range of weddings in a city like London with all its different cultures is a far more enriching experience than in Poland, where I first learned the trade," she explained, "though weddings there are also very festive and last many days."

As she talked, my eyes wandered around the open wardrobes bursting with further displays of pastel-coloured silk and satin dresses, surmounted by the flying saucer shapes of transparent tulle wedding hats hovering just beneath the ceiling. The male attire stood in one corner with a wide range of materials for ties and waistcoats, thus proving that male peacocks can be every bit as fastidious over their appearance as the traditional bride.

She does not just cover weddings in West London. She despatches wedding dresses as far as Romania, Kazakhstan and Thailand. She provides clothes for fashion shoots, christenings and commercial adverts but the bulk of her work is to serve the summer weddings. Her main dressmaker formerly sewed dresses for the fashion-conscious consort of Polish President Kwasniewski.

Originally a trained aromatherapist, Agata loves her new work. She calms wedding day nerves and remains friends with her clients for years after the wedding. Her biggest problem is to get bridal dress measurements right for pregnant brides racing to get their marriage certificate before the baby arrives. Polish priests discourage christening children of unmarried mothers so ladies abandon their libertarian lifestyle and get hitched. But at least they do it in style.

Ealing Gazette August 31st 2007

A New Polish University

A stone's throw from the QPR Stadium in Shepherds Bush is Phoenix High School. It has now become a prominent Polish landmark. Last year it became the site of a new Polish Saturday school with over a 100 Polish children attending classes in the Polish language, Polish history and geography.

Now the sight of all those well scrubbed Polish children milling around Bloemfontein Road will be supplemented by an older Polish student. In the last 3 weeks more than 100 young Polish workers, male and female (but mostly female!), have been registering for 3 year BA courses in English, management studies, communications technology and teacher training. They will be paying £1800 per year to the WHSE, the Academy of Economics and Humanities in Lodz, which has set up a branch in West London.

It seems amazing that hard-working young Polish waitresses, handymen, builders' mates and kitchen porters are prepared to eke out some of their hard-earned income to pay these not insubstantial fees and to find the spare time and the energy to drag their weary bleary-eyed bodies to face a series of weekend tutorials. Would they not prefer to sleep off their weekly toil in a comfy bed in their poky little flat?

"Firstly, our fees are far lower than what they would be paying for a place in an English University," says the WHSE's 25 year old International Projects Coordinator, Magdalena Biernat, who looks as young as the students.

"You must not underestimate the hunger for self-betterment that drives these young aspiring Poles to resume university studies that they had broken off in Poland in order to come to work in England. They don't want to serve tables for the next 5 years! The only question," this former drama student from Exeter University adds ruefully, "is whether they will they have the will power in their difficult circumstances to stay the course."

She was interviewing fellow lecturers from Poland during August and planning the inauguration ceremony in early October. She and her colleagues are determined that this opportunity to return to academic studies should also be enriched by close contact with other London nationalities so that young Poles can come out of their self-imposed shell and get to know other ethnic cultures.

Ealing Gazette – September 7th 2007

Exorcising the Polish Demons

Every month, as the sky darkens, a coven of female healers gather together in the eyrie on the top floor of the Polish Centre in Hammersmith. Their broomsticks have been replaced now by Oyster cards. These are the members of the newly formed Polish Psychologists Club.

In less than 2 years they have enrolled nearly 80 psychologists, special needs teachers and sociologists as members, though curiously only 3 of them are male. They discuss their career problems, monitor the latest legislation and academic trends affecting their profession and organize seminars, lectures and psychological advice columns for the "Polish Daily" and "Polish Express". They are now a member organization of the Federation of Poles in Great Britain and they have a written constitution longer than the Magna Carta.

Their biggest professional headache is the downgrading of their Polish masters' degrees by the NHS and by the British Psychological Society to only bachelor status, even though their Polish diplomas are recognized in full by British universities. However they are still able to practise their profession in the private sector unhindered. Their patients come from all walks of British life but many specialize in treating the specific problems of migrants and ethnic minorities.

A typical example of this entrepreneurial breed is glamorous looking 30 year old Agnieszka Major. (Major incidentally is a Polish surname and she is NOT related to the former British Prime Minister.) She graduated in Poland with a Masters Degrees in Law and Psychology. Already fluent in Spanish and Italian she came to London 4 years ago to learn English. Within 6 months she had set up NLP – Gate, her own consulting practice in Willesden. As a specialist in the business orientated field of Neurologistic Programming she has organized seminars, training and therapeutic group sessions for members of the East European Business Centre.

She considers herself to be a secular missionary working among Poles abroad to improve their quality of life. She sees two major psychological problems affecting her mostly male patients. Firstly, depression amongst those who feel they have not succeeded too well in an alien environment, and secondly, the intense loneliness and lack of self-fulfilment amongst many of those who HAVE succeeded professionally. It seems that both success and failure breed their own separate demons. Miss Major and her friends are there to provide the therapy to exorcise them.

Ealing Gazette September 14th 2007

Acton Park Festival for Peace

There were 12 stalls in Acton Park Community Festival last Sunday commemorating the Polish contribution to the London Week of Peace.

Polish families turned up several hundred strong to enjoy the last of the summer sun with children romping in the park while the adults mostly formed one long queue. Although there was a stall from Bronek's Delicatessen serving up hot steaming bigos and selling Polish delicacies, the Ministry of Transport trailer giving advice on transferring former Polish cars to UK registration numbers, a stall representing Western Union with their customary yellow balloons, the local East Acton Safer Neighbourhood Team, advice on membership from the GMB Union officials and a display of smiling pretty Polish-speaking policewomen fronting the Metropolitan Police stall, the queue formers ignored all these and wound their way right past the stall of a well-known solicitor's firm and terminating at the Citizens Advice Bureau alongside it. Understandably, the solicitors seemed to look a little miffed.

The CAB representative, John Oakes, a Haringey Councillor in his spare time, said that there was an enormous need for good free legal advice in Polish for new arrivals suffering discrimination and accidents at work, unscrupulous landlords, consumer fraud and racially motivated attacks. However he had not expected the uptake in Acton Park to be so large. Within the first three hours they had over 100 new cases reported to them. This need is exacerbated by the closure of the local CAB in Ealing. Curiously the CAB advice centre at the Acton festival, represented by John Oakes and Polish-speaking Bozena Krahn, was based not in West London at all, but in far away Enfield and covered the northern London Boroughs.

The initiative for this festival of community peace actually came from the Acton branch of the Metropolitan Police and specifically from its firefly of a Polish-speaking uniformed police officer - PWC Agnieszka Grzondziel. Agnieszka has only been in this country for 5 years but her enthusiastic and sustained contribution to improving relations between the local police and the new Polish arrivals has been invaluable. After all she speaks their language, and unlike perhaps some of the older Polish generations, she understands their idiomatic speech and knows what motivates them and what may lead to cultural misunderstanding in a strange foreign environment.

Ealing Gazette – September 21st 2007

Polish Station on the Airwaves

Polish radio in West London has undergone a vital upward step change. Radio Orla is emerging from the internet into the FM airwaves. It has linked up with Hayes FM radio to produce a 2 hour evening chat show every Saturday.

The show, which is emitted between 7 and 9pm on frequency 91.8 is a chat show run by bilingual Polish-born Lukasz Foster in both Polish and English. It plays popular Polish music but also comments on local and national events in this country. Lukasz does not have things all his own way. An obstreperous gatecrasher appears on each show calling himself Don Pedro and plays the devil's advocate to any seemingly sensible opinion that Lukasz expresses.

Despite the tomfoolery they include serious issues such as the coming Polish elections, the exploitation of Polish workers in England and an interview with world famous Polish architect Daniel Libeskind.

Sutish Sharma, the managing director of Hayes FM, explained to me that the cooperation between his radio station and Radio Orla has been going very well and he is hoping soon to expand the weekly Polish 2 hour slot to 4 hours. The Radio obtained a licence last year and opened on September 1st in the presence of local Hayes MP John McDonnell. It covers a 5 mile radius around Hayes, which takes in large swathes of the Boroughs of Ealing, Hillingdon and Hounslow. It has regular listeners in Hanwell and Greenford and a friend told me recently he heard it driving down South Ealing Road. It is a community radio with news updates and serious commentary as well as Asian and British music. "I tell all my listeners what a great area this is to live in and hope that more Poles come into this area," Sutish told me. He has a BBC background and Hayes FM has a joint project partner status with the BBC.

Teresa Sucharzewska, one of those British-born Poles (like me, but younger and prettier), is conducting a marketing strategy for Hayes FM. She expects to cover Polish events in London as well as ceremonies at the Polish War Memorial in Northolt. "We (Poles) have been in this country so long," she told me, "and yet no one really knows about us even though we had a Pope for 26 years".

Ealing Gazette – September 28th 2007

Elections are Coming

Election fever has gripped West London residents as the starting gun went off. They debate the dire choice between the clunking fist of the incumbent leadership and the disarray in the opposition parties.

No. I am not referring to Gordon Brown. That is very much a secondary consideration.

It is the Polish parliamentary elections that have caught the attention of West London Poles, both old and young. The fate of the gutsy incorruptible ruling twins, the Kaczynski brothers, one a President, the other the Prime Minister, is at stake. Their anti-corruption campaign and their challenge to the post-Communist Polish oligarchs have fired the imagination of the old Polish veterans who had been hostile to the Soviet puppet regime in Poland for half a century. On the other hand the Kaczynskis' confrontational style of government, their narrow 1950's mindset on social issues and their reliance on maverick extremists as coalition partners have embarrassed the younger Poles and made their country seem a laughing stock.

Polls show the leading parties in Poland are neck and neck. Both government and opposition have cast their eyes greedily on the 600,000 strong Polish electorate in Britain to tilt the balance. The Polish consulate has divided up the country into 16 electoral regions to accommodate this expatriate electorate.

Donald Tusk from the main liberal opposition party was the first leader to come to London. After photo-opportunities on Saturday at Polish war memorials in Northolt and Gunnersbury and at a Tesco Polish food counter, he addressed a loud and acrimonious hustings in the theatre at the POSK centre in Hammersmith. The room was heaving with mostly young and middle aged supporters, while a few elderly émigrés watched less enthusiastically from the front rows. One angry and persistent croaky-voiced heckler in the balcony however tried to make Tusk's life a misery as he accused him of condoning Communism and corruption.

Tusk concentrated on his main theme. "We want to look West for our models, not East", he said. "Why can't Poland be like Britain?" he added. "Then you can all come home."

Angry debates continued in the corridors and coffee bars. It promised to be a watershed election. No fence sitting here, I thought.

Outside I ran into some Polish friends and mentioned the election hustings. "Elections? What elections?" they asked.

Ealing Gazette – October 5th 2007

Agnieszka the Ambulance Hero

26 year old Agnieszka is employed along with 20 other fellow Poles as an ambulance driver. I said "employed" but actually she is a contracted free lancer working 10 hours a day, five days a week, without a break.

Despite the hours Agnieszka loves her job. A cheeky petite blonde with an impish smile, she has close empathy with all the patients she carries, despite language problems.

Her company is contracted to ferry cancer and kidney patients to the main hospitals in Ealing and Hammersmith. Their ambulances resemble police cars and Agnieszka recalls with amusement how approaching vehicles often dramatically reduce their speed until they spot the words "ambulance" and then accelerate again. However, she can drive in the bus lane and pays no congestion charge.

True, she also cannot speed. There is no blue lamp and no siren. However on one occasion she was stopped by a community police officer and asked to convey a drunk lying unconscious in the road. She sped with her precious and somewhat aromatic cargo to the A&E at Hammersmith Hospital and was asked by the duty doctor to give a diagnosis. "Look," she told the astonished doctor in her broken English, "I am not paramedic. I am only taxi driver for day patients."

On another occasion she was overtaken by a van with back doors swinging open. In her rear mirror she saw a man running after the van, yelling "That's my van! They've stolen it." So Agnieszka, ever the knight in shining armour, took the victim in her car and gave chase! The van owner rang the police on his mobile to report the crime and confirmed that he was in hot pursuit of the thieves in an ambulance.

"Put the siren on," the police told him. "Then give us the location and we'll join you."

"I can't," said Agnieszka, "I have no siren! I'm not an emergency ambulance."

Nevertheless she followed the stolen vehicle around the highways and byways of Ealing and Acton and finally chased the van into a cul de sac in the South Acton estate and boxed them in. There was a surreal scene as the two burly looking thieves got out the van, and confronted this lunatic young blonde driver who had just stepped out of her ambulance. They looked at each other and then ran off.

Lucky for Agnieszka that they did. She had been left on her own. It took the police nearly 15 minutes to arrive.

Her controller was not amused. Agnieszka's dedication to her job and her patients just leaves him cold.

Agnieszka has done a first aid course now. Her English is improving. Yet she has no opportunity to develop her career with her current outfit. She wants to sit the exam to be a paramedic and to work for the NHS direct. Hard decisions await her if she wants to better her lot.

Ealing Gazette – October 12th 2007

Poles are Serial Kissers.

Nowadays when young Polish men meet unexpectedly in the street a greeting requires a hug and a handshake. Maybe an occasional high five is exchanged. Some 50 years ago they would have stood and doffed their hats at each other with the distinctive courtesy of a Japanese bow but those elegant days are long gone.

If it is a female/female or a female/male greeting then hugging and kissing is almost obligatory. The older Pole may kiss an older lady's hand but that is not so common now. But kisses on cheeks are never resisted by the female recipient and she will be equally bound by custom to reciprocate. British air-kissing would be as alien to Poles as a limp handshake. Poles are oblivious to scare stories in Britain about kissing being in some way unhygienic or uncivilized. Old British traditions of kissing once at Christmas under a sprig of mistletoe would seem quite archaic. Poles seem to wear mistletoe over their heads 24/7.

In fact Polish ritual demands 3 kisses in a row on alternate cheeks. A single peck could be seen as a form of diplomatic disapproval, as in "I'm cross with you, so I'll only kiss you once!" That is the Polish equivalent of being sent to Coventry.

Children are kissed by adults on their foreheads but many kids find their gran's slobbering kisses a little embarrassing in front of their English school-friends.

A growing number of my fellow Londoners like this Polish tradition. They tend to seek out Polish company at, say, a posh Ealing Town Hall reception, in order to undergo this native Polish ritual, as quaint to them as a Maori nose greeting. Some, like our Polish-speaking MP Steve Pound, take to it like a duck to water channelling their touchy-feely bonhomie through to all their constituents the Polish way. It does not seem to have lost him any votes so far.

For British-born Poles like me it is a wonderful excuse. I can alternate between my British stiff upper lip reserve at public functions followed by the pleasure of kissing any attractive lady I come across. "That's OK," they say to their partners, "He's Polish, you know!" And their partners nod their heads resignedly.

Ealing Gazette – October 19th 2007

Poles take to the Polls

The 500 strong queue snaked its way in the bright autumn sun of last Sunday from the side entrance to the Polish Centre, under the railway bridge and deep into Ravenscourt Park. Puzzled British passers-by wondered what they were lining up to buy. Actually they were queuing to vote.

Never before had I seen queues like this for any British election. 8238 Poles (overwhelmingly young and below the age of 35) had registered to vote at the POSK Centre, and a further 60,000 had registered in 20 other polling stations throughout the UK.

I joined the end of the queue in the park. Some who arrived took one look at the queue and left. Others resigned themselves reluctantly to waiting, and Poles being Poles were soon chatting and joking. Next to me there was a family from Hemel Hempstead, an old gent from Slough and a young woman teacher from Ealing. A young couple entertained us with poems lampooning Poland's politicians. It took us two hours to finally reach the polling booths but by that time it was a carnival atmosphere as people bought coffees and sandwiches for each other and stood in for those rushing to the loo.

To add to the colour local MP Greg Hands entertained those queuing with a welcoming handshake and a Conservative Party leaflet.

So few of the young people had bothered to vote when in Poland but here in England, concerned by Poland's appalling international image, they were determined to make a change. I found precious few sympathisers of the ruling Kaczynski twins in my section of the queue.

A hundred people at a time were allowed into the polling station, divided alphabetically into four columns. A group of 11 volunteers led by a tireless Ewa Brzeska, on duty since 5am, checked the names off the registers and handed each voter a voting slip for the Senate as well as what looked a giant paper tablecloth. This latter document proved to be the voting sheet for the local Warsaw MP.

When the polls closed at 8pm the heroic 11 stayed incarcerated in the building. Armed with rubber bands and black coffees, they stayed up all night counting the 5397 votes. They announced the results at 9.30 the next morning. A crushing defeat for the government and a well deserved sleep for the volunteers.

Ealing Gazette October 26th 2007

The "Indeks" Collectors

The students came in two by two as their names were called.

They sauntered up the stairs and across the stage where the two academics dressed in their chains of office and colourful regalia awaited them. Each of the 50 young men and 200 young women received their much coveted green covered student record book, the so-called "indeks".

In Poland these books are the student's main source of identity. They contain your photo, your personal data, your courses and your exam results and they accompany you everywhere. Here in England the "indeksy" and the academic robes were a reminder to these young Poles that there is a life outside the alien London environment of offices, kitchens, building sites and internet cafes. It was a life they had had to sacrifice when they first came to find better paid jobs in England.

Now, like some Noah's Ark, the Academy of Humanities and Economics had appeared from the Polish city of Lodz, to scoop them back into a familiar cultural environment and made them feel like valued members of society again.

After the applicants stood to attention to take their oath to be good and diligent students, the deputy Vice-Chancellor for the Academy's External and Non-Residential Studies, Dr Jacek Cheda, made a 20 minute address in which he recognized both the sacrifice and the sense of opportunity that persuaded these young people to part with £150 a month for upto 3 years and devote their spare time to obtain degrees in Information Technology, Management, English Philology or Educational Studies that would be recognized when they return to Poland. He also told them that they were part of the student body of one of Poland's largest educational establishments and reminded them of the "social" advantages of student life.

At this, the largely female audience sized up the "social" prospects of the handful of male students sitting timidly amongst them.

At the conclusion of this academic inauguration ceremony in the large Assembly Hall of Phoenix High School near White City, the new students gossiped and relaxed in the bright autumn sunshine which welcomed them to their new “campus”. Then, armed with their “indeksy” and with hearts and hopes uplifted, they departed for their opening lectures.

Ealing Gazette November 2nd 2007

Polish Children at Oldfield

Four young 6 year olds looked up at me expectantly as I entered the room with headmistress Elizabeth Day. I sat down quietly and within a minute the children had forgotten about my presence. I was just part of the pint-sized furniture.

Their teacher, Mrs Bozenna Kart, asked the children to introduce themselves one by one. They gave their names, the size of their families, their home address (including the postcode) and what kind of games and food they liked or disliked. Each made the statement "I speak English and…." And then each added a separate language. The young girl spoke Polish, the boys spoke Italian, Farsi and Tamil respectively. They had to read out different letters and simple English words based on pictures, spelled out different words thrown at them at random by their teacher and, as I quietly left them, they were preparing their own version of Little Red Riding Hood.

I was in one of the huts adjoining Oldfield Primary School playground in Greenford. The 4 youngsters belong to that substantial group of children in London who start school unable to speak English. At present nearly 50 such children in Oldfield need special extra induction classes to familiarize them with the English language and customs. Mrs Kart spends 3 days a week conducting classes with 4 or 5 children in each mixed group. Polish children form the largest contingent. There are 38 Polish pupils out of a school total of 317. This is not an exceptional figure for an Ealing non-denominational school but Catholic schools tend to have more. As many as 1277 children in Ealing's state schools speak Polish at home.

While the induction classes require time and resources there is little evidence that Ealing schools suffer in the long run. New cultures broaden the horizon of all the children. Oldfield's record for its year 6 pupils was outstanding this year making it the third best in the Borough.

Certainly most of the Polish mothers I spoke to seemed very pleased with the school. None of this surprises me. 55 years ago I went to a school in Ealing and speaking only Polish. Now I write a column every week in

English for the "Gazette" and the editor has not complained about my spelling so far.

Ealing Gazette – November 9th 2007

All Souls Day

South Ealing Cemetery. The Sunday following All Soul's Day. I am visiting my parents' grave.

On that day, the city of the dead becomes the garden of the living. Polish families, including grannies and young children, invade the graveyard armed with buckets, brushes, gardening tools and votive candles. They spread out along the rugged terrain, slipping on the muddy leaves and moving dexterously between the tombstones as they seek the monument that covers their loved ones. Fat squirrels and magpies scatter at the commotion but the black crows stay perched on the higher tombstones like dark sentinels from another world.

Here they all lie: Polish poets and generals, counts and peasants, priests and architects, teachers and craftsmen. They lived and died in Ealing. Yet their places of birth often denote some distant esoteric corner of an old pre-war Poland that is no more.

I watch the other families. First a quick prayer, and then they brush away the wet autumn leaves and clean the mud and dirt off the lettering on the tomb. With the tombs washed down, new bushes are planted and candles lit. Mourners pull out their folded canvass chairs and greet friends visiting neighbouring graves.

They await the procession at 3pm from the Polish church. It turns up, headed by three priests. Hundreds walk the cemetery perimeter as the graves are blessed. The sound of Hail Marys and the smell of incense waft across the silent necropolis.

Similar scenes had taken place at Gunnersbury Cemetery. There, in the previous week, a group of young enthusiasts from the Poland Street Association, organized by their Chairman, Michal Porzyczkowski, volunteered to identify and clean up some 300 tombs of forgotten Polish and British war heroes, often with no families to mourn them and with dilapidated crumbling tombstones. These selfless new arrivals from Poland, washed each tombstone, lighted lamps of remembrance and placed a Polish flag and a Union Jack on each tomb. It was a poignant reminder of a joint comradeship of arms in a distant past.

No frivolous American-style Hallowe'en masks here in South Ealing. Memory and quiet reflection are the order of the day. We stand in silence while busy traffic roars past the outer cemetery gates.

Ealing Gazette – November 16th 2007

After Independence Day

For Poles, nearly every month in the year evokes a mood.

You mention January and it's the grim rebellion of 1863; September (1939) - the cataclysmic invasion of Poland by Hitler and Stalin; March, June, October and December are associated with upheavals against Communist rule (the years were 1968, 1976, 1956 and 1970 respectively); May is a joyous month that celebrates Europe's first written constitution published in Warsaw in 1791 (we even beat the French to it!); August is a mixture of tears and joy as it covers the emergence of the independent Solidarity union (1980) and victory over the Bolsheviks (1920), but also the Warsaw Uprising of 1944 when a quarter of a million Poles perished and the Nazis destroyed Warsaw.

November is a month of sombre joy. November 11th is Independence Day. The year was 1918. The First World War was over. Amid the post-war devastation from marching Russian, German and Austrian armies, in which thousands of young Polish conscripts had perished, the former patriotic revolutionary, Jozef Pilsudski, returned to Warsaw from a German prison, to assume the presidency of a new independent Poland which had been wiped off the map 123 years before.

Poles in West London celebrated the event with a mass at St Andrew's church and a ceremony at the POSK centre in Hammersmith. The enthusiastic 28 year old events organizer for the Poland Street Association, Robert Nowakowski, had arranged a computer link up with their sister organization in Belfast, and used the charming old Pilsudski Institute adjoining POSK to hold a joint remembrance ceremony involving all the leading figures of the older Polish community. It was an extraordinary and uplifting bonding event between the old steadfasts and the brash new arrivals.

It was followed by a celebration in the POSK theatre, laid on by the Federation of Poles in Great Britain. An hour long lecture by Poland's chief archivist, Dr Tadeusz Krawczak, gave new insights into those heroes of 1918 who carried the flame of independence right through to the independent Solidarity Congress in Gdansk barely 62 years later. Then an evocative and lusty musical celebration of Poland's historic struggles sung by the Ave Verum Choir from Croydon, brought to life even those who might have nodded off during the earlier lecture.

Ealing Gazette November 23rd 2007

Polish YMCA

Were you watching the Lord Mayor's Show on telly? Did you see the prancing hobby-horse? This strange 800 year old Polish mythical creature had appeared for the first time in the equally ancient 750 year history of the Lord Mayor's Show. Surrounded by the bright costumes of his dance troupe, the "horse" explained to the interviewer the story of the courageous trumpeter of Krakow with the Tartar arrow through his throat. Former Old Dunstanians from Gunnersbury RC School would have immediately recognized the "horse" as their old teacher Wlodek Lesiecki.

Wlodek is the artistic director of the formidable 120 strong "Mazury" Dance Company, whose 60th Anniversary will be celebrated at the Southbank next year.

I met him at a large mansion on Gunnersbury Avenue. With its front porch surmounted by a Polish eagle, the building is actually the HQ for the Polish YMCA, which had been operating in London continuously since the War especially after it was banned by the Communists in Poland.

"Mazury" is an integral part of the Polish YMCA and one of the many activities in which second and third generation Polish boys and girls in London, of all ages, can nurture their Polish sensibilities in physically active and culturally enhancing events like the popular summer camps abroad and the globe-trotting kids from the School of Masters Karate and Kickboxing Club. There is also a ladies volleyball team and an extreme sports club, whose 20 year old head-bangers indulge in paragliding, diving from rocks and other hare brained hobbies.

The two front rooms of the YMCA are festooned with challenge cups, diplomas, pre-war and wartime badges as well as numerous photographs of dancers in colourful costumes, black belted kids in white pyjamas at a kickboxing championship in Romania and young mountain hikers.

The Polish YMCA Director, Andy Lowczynowski, is the former coach of the England Women's Volleyball team. The continued success of this organization relies on the professionalism of such managers, its ability to develop leadership skills among its younger members and its uncloying easy-going Polish feel-good factor which is attractive to both the traditional Polish families and the new arrivals. "Many of our young kids," explained Wlodek, "come from totally different backgrounds and yet here the magic will happen as old and new weld together."

Ealing Gazette – November 30th 2007

A Polish Internet TV Station

I loved watching them as they sat provocatively in their long dresses on the lawn near the Albert Memorial or snuggled up together on a sofa, telling each other the most outrageous scraps of the news from the world press. Amidst girlish giggles Paulina Tralewska and Daria Paternoga describe delicious little morsels of scandal with an air of skittish naivety and pouting innocence.

It was these programmes that got me hooked on PL-TV, the first Polish language internet television station in London. Although a whole programme lasts only for one hour each week (every Thursday at 8pm) it contains a lot more serious information than just this saucy gossip. For instance a reporter from Radio Orla reads a weekly news bulletin. There is a summary of literary and theatrical reviews, as well as sound advice given by Polish-speaking experts on investing hard earned money, or setting up a business or bank account or on employment and tenant rights. Recent programmes included interviews with the newly elected Polish prime minister and with a popular Polish comic actor.

Last weekend PL-TV celebrated its first birthday. Paulina and Daria, as alluring as ever, greeted us at the entrance with glasses of white wine amidst the laid-back comfort of the Jazz Café at the POSK Centre in Hammersmith. Meanwhile the crème de la crème of the young newly arrived professionals, such as bankers, insurance agents, accountants, restaurateurs and shop owners, joined in for a concert and a relaxed chat.

The TV producer and controller, Tomasz Tyranowicz, an experienced photographer and a Greenford resident, introduced a short history of the station and explained the plans for the future. For two months now PL-TV has been cooperating with the Eye TV group. From January next year it will be available on one of the Sky channels. Though other enterprises are entering this field, PL-TV remains the pioneer.

The programmes are targeted at 18 to 35 year olds. They are firmly directed at young Poles who feel sufficiently well off to respond to lifestyle advertising campaigns, including credit card promotions, adventure holidays, tailor-made clothes, quality bakers and restaurants.

As long as Paulina and Daria continue to front TV-PL in their inimitable style I cannot see it failing.

Ealing Gazette December 7th 2007

A Meeting of Mayors

We stood in a huddle with our soaked umbrellas at the windswept Civic Amenity Site in Greenford (or "the Greenford dump" according to my taxi driver!).

We must have looked a sorry sight as we shivered in our child-sized yellow safety jackets. We were listening to the Polish-speaking staff at the site and from the adjoining Ealing Community Transport as they briefed Mayor Zbigniew Dubiel and Council leader Michal Sikorski from the green and leafy Warsaw District of Bielany on Ealing's waste and recycling practices. As Mr Sikorski is somewhat of an XL bulky size, reminiscent perhaps of his opposite number in Ealing, the safety jacket streamed from his left shoulder like a linesman's scarf. It was a necessary if less exuberant phase in the Polish Mayor's visit to Ealing but our Ealing Mayor, Mrs Hazel Ware, stood there under her brolly grinning from ear to ear.

As well she should! For this was her triumph as Mayor. She was the one with the soft spot for Ealing's Polish links. She had greeted the newly elected Polish Prime Minister with a hug and kiss in November and obtained the promise that during his next UK visit he will return to Ealing Town Hall. It was she who convinced her cost-cutting colleagues on Ealing Council that Ealing should honour its charter twinning agreements with Marcq en Baroeul in France and Bielany in Poland and resuscitate its connections with both districts.

The Polish visit may only have lasted three days but during that time the Mayor and Council Leader visited a school, toured Perceval House, were received at the Havelock Gurdwara, attended meetings on housing, education and the working of the Council Steering Group, enjoyed a whirlwind tour of London including a flight on London Eye, celebrated mass at Ealing Abbey and experienced pub lunches and a tandoori supper.

Local Polish community leaders collected the guests from Luton Airport and attended and assisted at all of these events, but Polish-speaking Ealing Councillor Joanna Dabrowska, in particular, came into her own, as she charmed and shepherded the Polish guests around these events with her inimitable chirpy bonhomie.

The Polish guests departed exhausted but happy and keen to have Ealing's officials paying an equally instructive return visit to Bielany.

Ealing Gazette – December 14th 2007

A Modern Nativity Play

In the end it was bound to happen. Climate change has hit the Nativity Play. The starry-eyed children grouped around the manger sang a cheerful song about waiting for Santa and his presents. But according to the song there was no snow now and he could not use his sleigh. So he had to pass a driving test in order to carry the children's presents by car down the motorway. The children cheerfully delivered this upbeat yuletide message followed by the famous Polish lullaby carol to Jesus which uses a richer confection of affectionate words of endearment than any Shakespearean love sonnet.

We were listening to the Christmas message voiced by children at the John Paul II Polish Saturday school on the site of Phoenix High School near White City. The headmistress, Irena Grocholewska, a redoubtable elderly lady who is also Chair of the Polish Teachers Union in the UK, reminded everyone that the school was now into its second year with 150 children attending between the ages of 5 and 16.

The parents pay £70 per term and a group of volunteer parents attend as minders all day. The teachers are professionals from Poland. Children are taught Polish literature, history, geography and maths. Maths? Why maths?

"Unlike most of the other Polish Saturday schools in London," Mrs Grocholewska explained, "this one is geared towards children whose parents expect to return to Poland some day. Polish children need to know basic mathematical terms in their language if they continue their schooling in Poland."

At the senior end they prepare children for Polish school diplomas and not, like other Polish schools, for GCSEs and A levels in Polish. A recent visit by Polish Ministry of Education officials endorsed their teaching programme.

Local MP Andrew Slaughter, who also attended the Christmas concert, was equally impressed and not just by the delicious cakes and the Christmas card he received from the children. He admired the determination and enthusiasm with which the school was run. He remarked on how polite the children were when they stood up for him and wished him Merry Christmas in English as he visited each class.

"The school deserves a financial grant from a British source," said the MP, a former Leader of Hammersmith Council, "if only as a token of appreciation for their splendid work."

Ealing Gazette – December 21st 2007

A Polish Christmas Eve

It is Christmas Eve. The crisp cold air adds magic to the evening. The Christmas tree has just been decorated with lights, honeycake and shiny baubles. (No self-respecting Polish family erects their tree earlier than December 23rd - it would be like celebrating Easter during the middle of Lent.) While mum and her friends bustle in the kitchen and her partner lines up the bottles, young Luiza has a special task to perform. She watches the darkening sky from the window, waiting for the first star to appear, supposedly the star of Bethlehem.

Once the star is spotted Luiza runs downstairs and her screams of delight are the starting gun for a Polish Christmas. All the guests, even the reluctant teenagers, indulge in a typical Polish "kiss-wish-fest" as they break their sacred wafers ("oplatki") with each other and wish each and all wealth and health. Then, fortified with wine and rounds of vodka, the convivial gathering seats itself expectantly around the white table cloth with an underlay of straw "from the stable".

On this festive "work-bench" we begin our Herculean task of consuming 12 servings of the richest dishes imaginable. Smoked herring in cream, fish soup and beetroot soup with ear-shaped dumplings are euphemistically called starters. Then the revellers go for the big game: the royal carp first cooked, then in aspic, then fried, then in batter. Other exotic dishes include cabbage leaves stuffed with rice and pasta sprinkled with poppyseed, but not a sliver of meat among them. After all this is the final pre-Christmas fast! The dried fruit compotes and walnut rolls warn us that the battle is nearly over and we can change our drink from vodka to coffee.

An interval for a quiet after-dinner nap and then for the whoops of laughter as we draw the presents from under the tree and see what our nearest and dearest decided that we want for Christmas.

After this the mass migration begins to St Andrew's Church for the midnight Mass. Like the vast herds of wildebeest that roam the Serengeti plains braving the crocodile-infested rivers, inebriated Polish families risk police patrols as they drive to join the overflowing church congregations. Here we pelt out our traditional carols filling the church with the unmistakable fumes of our Christmas spirit.

There's nothing like a Polish Christmas.

Ealing Gazette - December 28th 2007

The Flight to Warsaw

With a roar of engines the metal bird departed Heathrow and plunged into the sky. The back of the Airbus, where I was sitting, shook and clattered in the tailwind. We held on grimly and silently until we reached the steadier cruising stream high above the clouds.

Just two days before the New Year, the plane was not as crowded as during the pre-Christmas weeks, the BA stewardess explained.

Widow Alicja Krakowiecka (In her early sixties? Sorry, Alicja!) had just come back from an enjoyable 2 weeks spent with her Polish friends in Hanwell. It was her first visit to London. She had loved the London Eye and the West End shops, and enjoyed an exquisite ex-pat Polish Christmas. Now she was travelling back to her small coastal town of Kolobrzeg to see in the New Year nursing her new glam granny English hairdo.

A boisterous bunch of young Scottish-born Londoners (largely from Stamford Brook apparently) were ready to try out Warsaw for a Hogmanay bar crawling experience. "We've done Spain every year for the last 3 years. Now we want to try something different," one of them explained.

I assured them it would be different. Daytime temperatures fell below zero and snow was predicted for New Years Eve. "And don't wear kilts," I warned them. "For two reasons: first, frostbite under the sporran is not pleasant and, secondly, while Poles do have a sense of humour, they fail to see the funny side of Brits in kilts vomiting and mooning outside a church."

I ran into my old friend Michal Dembinski, a former Perivale resident and President of the Anglo-Polish Chamber of Commerce, now returning to Warsaw with his children after spending Christmas with his family in Manchester. "It's now less of a paying proposition for Poles to travel to

England to work. The pound is so weak against the Polish zloty," he explained. Michal told me he was holding a conference next April on whether Poland should join the euro and can no longer find a speaker supporting an immediate currency conversion.

We agreed we could ask this question of our friend who is the new Polish Finance Minister. After all Minister Jacek Rostowski is UK born and still has a home in Earls Court. Yet another Polish West Londoner.

So fly BA to Warsaw, folks. All West London flies with you!

Ealing Gazette – January 4th 2008

Polish Beauties in Riverside

Who wants to see the five most beautiful women from Poland?

Not far to go. Just saunter down to the Riverside Studios near Hammersmith Bridge each Wednesday at 6.30 from now until February 6th and you are in for a treat.

The Studios have teamed up with the Polish Cultural Institute to lay on film evenings each Wednesday which will feature what the Institute has called "some of the most legendary Polish beauties to have graced the big screen."

First in line was the vampish silent movie screen star Pola Negri who appeared in Polish and German films before moving to Hollywood in 1920. She appeared on Wednesday in two films. In the first, "The Beast", made in 1917, she was a brainy beauty who unwittingly ensnares a bandit who in turn abandons his own family to follow her. Even wilder was the second film "Sumurun" where she played an exotic beauty who divides up another family, when a sheikh falls out with his own son over this Polish femme fatale.

Pola Negri's films reflected her real life. Her vampish style suited the silent film studios in the twenties and ensnared Valentino and Chaplin. Once the talkies came her strong Polish accent and her passionate form of acting put off a more puritanical 1930's American audience. I still remember her though as an elegant older lady in Disney's "Moonspinners" with Hayley Mills. She died aged 93.

Next Wednesday the aristocratic Beata Tyszkiewicz herself introduces the classic 1969 Polish film "The Doll", in which she plays an empty-headed snobbish aristocrat who strings along a rich and naïve businessman and leads him to self-destruction.

On January 23rd a sultry Grazyna Szapolowska also appears in person to introduce her two films from the 1980s. In one she plays a seductive Hungarian journalist and in the other, directed by Kieslowski, she seduces a young boy who spies on her other lovers.

On January 30th Magdalena Cielecka is a younger seductress, a Gwynneth Paltrow look alike. As a nun she tempts a famous Cardinal and informs on him to his Communist captors. In her second film she plays a wife who falls for an older man on a boat trip. Lucky him! She too will appear in person.

For more details on these dangerous Polish sirens check the Institute's website – www.polishculture.org.uk

Ealing Gazette – January 11th 2008

The Polish Legal Centre

Every Tuesday evening, a stream of unhappy Poles pours into the POSK building in Hammersmith looking for free legal advice. They have come to consult the Polish Legal Centre.

A young female volunteer sits at a small table next to the central pillar. She takes note of the details, asks the visitor to take a seat in the vestibule and notifies the Centre staff upstairs of their arrival. Presently they are asked to take a lift to the second floor and then turn right towards the Green Room (or the "Sapphire Room" as it is often grandiosely called). Here they are introduced to a striking raven-haired young lady. She is Maryia Abdul, a legal expert on hire to the Centre from the charity Law for All. She is accompanied by a Polish interpreter while another staff member takes notes. The visitors settle down and present their burning problems.

Dark tales of exploitation, injustice and insensitivity cross the counselling table, week in week out. Tenant expulsions, unfair dismissals, back-breaking work for less than the legal minimum wage, discrimination and sexual harassment in the office, bullying and fraudulent cash payments... All are exposed here.

Clients pour out their sorrows and seek solutions during these two hour Tuesday sessions. The relevant application forms are completed and legal advice is dispensed free of charge. Trickier cases are passed on to the Law for All head office. The only requirement is that the visitor calls in advance to book a session and to give the Legal Centre team a brief description of their grievance.

The initiative for this worthwhile venture came from City legal worker Gabriel Olearnik. The Director of the Centre is another City colleague, an earnest looking bespectacled Marcin Perzanowski. "We need more sponsorship to continue and to expand this vital work," he told me.

At least 25 unpaid volunteers take turns to assist at these sessions. I was very impressed by the sense of solidarity that motivated these successful young number-crunchers and legal eagles of the Polish City Club, barely new arrivals from Poland themselves, to devote so much time and effort to help their less fortunate fellow countrymen.

To book an appointment with the Polish Legal Centre please ring 0208 600 3100

Ealing Gazette – January 18th 2008

The Age of the Polish Plumber

On Friday I went in search of that mythical beast passed on from one British middle class housewife to another with all the secrecy evinced by Catholic families when smuggling recusant priests across Elizabethan England. Two years ago this creature had symbolized the successful "Non" vote in the French EU referendum.

I refer of course to the Polish plumber. Over the last 3 years this magnificent species seems to have replaced most of its natural rivals just as the grey squirrel has replaced the red variety in our glorious English countryside.

My wife complained about the water pressure in our house. I was entrusted with the delicate mission of finding one of these elusive creatures somewhere in their traditional Northolt habitat.

My quest led me to Carr Road, possibly the longest residential road in Ealing Borough. Here I ran down Darek, a shy hard-working young man who had taken up the trade in 2004 as soon as Poland had joined the EU. He is a registered self-employed and applying to join the Institute of Plumbing and Heating Engineers.

In truth Darek has never had to advertise his business as plumber or general handyman. Working sometimes with his father in law, but mostly on his own, he has found constant work simply by being recommended by word of mouth first with Polish families and later from one English household to another. For instance, after completing a decorating job and some garden decking for a famous BBC radio interviewer near Ravenscourt Park, he then built a garden shed/studio for his sculptor neighbour. Recently he has redecorated a new house in Marlow and constructed an office in a garden shed in Acton.

He puts his success down to being quick, neat and flexible to his clients' requests, even though he still cannot understand why some traditional British householders still prefer separate hot and cold taps and still use wallpaper. His English is not fluent but he has never failed to understand his clients while his bank employs Polish staff.

He thinks Polish plumbers deserve their good reputation although rogues exist. "Only take tradesmen on recommendation and make sure they come in punctually and with clean tools," is his advice.

And my water pressure problem? Well, a bit busy for now. Can he come in April?!

Ealing Gazette – January 25th 2008

Let There Be Love

"Why don't you go back to the Czech Republic?" the cantankerous old immigrant from Grenada yelled at his home help.

"How dare you!" she yelled. "Can't you see I'm Polish?"

"Well, to me you all look the same," he retorted gruffly.

The largely black audience in the Tricycle Theatre hooted with embarrassed laughter at this exchange. Yet amidst the tears of mirth at this crackling dialogue, the audience, of whatever skin colour, had much to reflect on.

We were watching Kwame Kwei-Armah's comedy drama "Let There be Love" built around the curmudgeonly character of a black Alf Garnett type, ranting on about white racism, Indian doctors, Eastern European immigrants and aggressive youths. Finally he warms to a perky young Polish housekeeper imposed on him by his daughters while continuously criticizing her foreign accent.

In a sense this cheeky play could potentially help lance a boil that is slowly festering here in Ealing and Hammersmith. Street brawls on Uxbridge Road and incidents in secondary schools are but the outward manifestation of an unspoken tension between some of the new Central European arrivals and some of the former immigrant communities.

No one will admit this officially though the police remain concerned. I know I am walking on egg-shells here, but the Polish presence is known to cause resentment amongst some local residents and this includes other national minorities. Journalist Yasmin Alibhai-Brown has even called the Poles "the new blacks".

On their arrival here nothing surprised the younger workers and pupils from rural Poland more than the multiethnic character of West London. They had no experience of meeting other races at home. They need a cultural guide through the minefield of race relations, almost as much as they need to learn English.

Such a cultural bridge is being built successfully for younger Polish children in our primary schools but teenagers in secondary schools of whatever colour are apt to listen to other voices. Some may harbour traditional preconceptions against other races. Other misunderstandings can occur too. Polish children are taught for instance that it is impolite to avoid eye contact but here others can interpret that as aggression.

Actually Poles do not share the guilt of many white Brits about their colonial past. Poles had no colonies. For 200 years they themselves were invaded, occupied and humiliated in the same way as Irish, Africans and Asians. So when challenged by outsiders young Poles can have the same sense of hurt and vulnerability as their black schoolmates and the same obstinate pride and determination not to lose face.

Perhaps, the first step towards a mutual respect and understanding between teenage Poles and blacks would be a joint school outing to see the play. If they can laugh together then they can coexist and work together. "Let There be Love" is a universal theme.

Ealing Gazette – February 8th 2008

Electing a Mayor for London

With trepidation I entered the Bridge Room on the fourth floor of the POSK Centre in Hammersmith.

I had heard that one of the brash new groups of young Polish executives, called the Polish Professionals, had been pushing the sceptical old guard in the Polish umbrella organization – the Federation of Poles in Great Britain – into organizing a press conference on the coming London elections for all the Polish media outlets in London. Chairman Jan Mokrzycki could sense the enthusiasm of his young brood. Overcoming the natural scepticism of his Federation colleagues he agreed to give the youngsters their conference.

I opened the door and edged quietly in to the darkened room. The next second, with an almighty clang, I tripped over a TV arc light. Sshhhh! Every one looked round as I struggled to my feet and the cameraman hastened to recover his equipment.

To my surprise, the room was packed to the gunnels. There were 3 TV crews and numerous young Polish journalists scribbling notes or holding their mikes forward.

Facing them was a large screen and two young presenters in their twenties, Adam Komarnicki and Malgorzata Krumplewska, taking it in turns, to enthuse their sympathetic audience with the need to promote the electoral registration of all Polish nationals throughout the UK, but specifically in London. They flashed statistics, EU legislation details, application forms, and a sexy looking logo with a voting card designed in the colours of the Polish flag being thrust into the slot of a Union Jack-covered box. "It looks like a penetration," said a shocked member of the audience accusingly. "Quite," others quickly agreed, giggling with approval.

The electoral enfranchisement campaign was called "Poles to Polls." There were 59,386 Polish nationals already on London's electoral registers. Add to that a further 5,000 names which Brent Council had failed to extrapolate, plus some 15,000 British citizens of Polish origin and you have a Polish electorate in London larger than a parliamentary constituency. "And of course that's not enough," said Adam, "There are many thousands more Poles in London unaware they have a right to vote." "There would be enough to swing the vote in a narrow contest," added Malgorzata. The audience cheered them.

Yes, the candidates have noticed too! Ken Livingstone will appear on a YouTube video for Polish voters and Boris Johnson is coming to the POSK Centre in March to speak to the Polish community. Poles will be anxious to support a candidate that can guarantee a Polish Festival next year in Trafalgar Square and they will be looking to see how much the newly elected (or re-elected) Mayor will listen to their problems. "They should listen to us," said Adam Komarnicki, "we all pay Council Tax and we are Polish Londoners now."

Ealing Gazette - 14th March 2008

Poles and the NHS

"Well you see, dahling," said my Polish countess friend as we sat together, drinking large tumblers of her Whisky and Coke in her West Ealing mansion, "we Poles are such hypochondriacs. We read up on all possible diseases, every small cold is potentially pneumonia, and when we visit the doctor we expect to confirm what we have already decided that we have. And if the doctor does not agree then we think he's a jerk."

I was sceptical but I had to admit that, despite her age, the careful Countess was the epitome of health and still able to parade proudly on a naturist beach.

But Polish women, young and old, read health magazines more avidly than any other subject. They tend to eat slowly and avoid junk food so they are not so obsessed with their figure. The occasional Rubenesque love handles are not really a matter of concern. But they are experts on every possible ailment imaginable and they know their health problems inside out, as well as that of their children and reluctant menfolk. When my wife scolds me sufficiently into going to a doctor on my own over some minor ailment or other she briefs me on my own symptoms and tests me to make sure I have remembered them correctly.

Polish ladies' coffee morning chit-chat would put many an international medical conference to shame. When they visit a doctor they go enriched with the communal knowledge of their friends and ready to challenge anything they hear. They analyse their prescriptions with meticulous detail, cross check on their Polish women's forum website, and then discard those they disapprove of before even reaching the chemist.

However in the UK they feel particularly frustrated because the GP system is calculated to frustrate their expertise. In Poland when they feel ill they visit an expert on the disease they have already adopted. In the UK you cannot see an expert on the NHS unless you are referred by a GP.

"But these GPs know nothing," one of my wife's friends complained, "they pretend to listen, don't even look at your tongue and then prescribe a painkiller for everything." I protest at this exaggeration but her friends dart in thick and fast and bury me with woeful tales of wrong diagnoses by "negligent" GPs with potentially lethal consequences which are finally resolved when they visit their former local hospital in Poland.

Actually many of the new Poles are unable to register at all with GPs, not only because of language difficulties, but because receptionists still insist on the production of two utility bills. For many Polish youngsters, hot-bedding in crowded tenements, this is impossible. So, at the slightest pain or strain, they invade the A&E sections of local hospitals and then fume at the long wait as other more deserving accident patients go ahead of them.

Polish patient and British doctor still do not mix as well as my friend's Whisky and Coke.

Ealing Gazette - 11th April 2009

Lady in charge of POSK

The Polish Social and Cultural Centre in Hammersmith, which we all call "POSK", has just undergone a sea change. The grim fortress-like building in King Street with its grey balconies but welcoming wide front entrance has allowed a wind of change to sweep through its many corridors. For the first time in its 40 year history it has elected a woman president. Hillary Clinton, don't give up yet!

Like her avuncular predecessor Olgierd Lalko, the new President, Ewa Brzeska, is a child of the old Polish veterans' generation that had once dominated Polish London society. Certainly a charismatic figure with her magical smile and soft but authoritative voice which had enchanted the children she once taught at Villiers High School, she oozes femininity and warmth through every fibre of her generously proportioned being. She is well prepared for her task both by her upbringing and her experience as a voluntary worker and she had been General Secretary of POSK for three years.

The meeting at which she was elected last Saturday was an exceptionally well attended 7 hour marathon with a 15 minute break. More than 330 people stayed till the end participating in the AGM of this Polish bastion of democracy, alternatively roused by provocative speeches and dozing through the more boring reports. Attempts to skip the democratic formalities through voting "by poll" were firmly brushed aside as Ewa and her newly elected Council obtained a clear mandate to clear out the cobwebs of POSK's 40 year constitution. The membership fee fixed back in 1967 had been a single lifetime payment of only £10. It needs to be upgraded and changed to an annual payment.

She has promised that more cobwebs would be cleared out. "Armed only with a pencil" she has promised to locate savings which will reduce POSK's current running deficit, maintain the vital modernization programme of POSK's facilities and assess whether POSK can afford a paid Chief Executive.

Ever mindful of the need to draw in new visitors and members from the recently arrived Polish diaspora she has promised to find the facilities around the POSK site for a crèche, and perhaps eventually a nursery. The pitter-patter of tiny feet around POSK's nooks and crannies may fill some of the older sedate members with dread, but there is already a popular children's theatre company, Syrena, which regularly uses the building and the crèche will bring young parents into more contact with the older institution. Those children could guarantee the social and the commercial future of POSK and, with all her respect for the older generation of POSK's founding fathers, it is on this new generation, as well as on her own, that the new POSK President's eyes are firmly fixed.

Ealing Gazette - 16th May 2008

Watching the Europe Match

The new Polish pub in West Ealing, the "Pan Tadeusz", was packed. I made my way in past the motley group of smokers standing on the pavement outside.

Inside, there were six plasma screens around the bar displaying the Poland-Croatia match and the young Polish audience were glued to their seats or leaning attentively behind those lucky enough to have seats. At least the Polish commentary did not torture the Polish surnames. There were copies of "Polski Sun" strewn over the tables. "The Sun", the lip-readers' digest, had taken a gamble on publishing in Polish during the Europe tournament. The news, the sports reports and even the page 3 girls were Polish.

Surprisingly, about a third of the fans in the pub were young women, some with the red and white Polish colours daubed on their cheeks. Periods of quiet concentration were interspersed with choruses of shouting as the Polish forwards hurled themselves fruitlessly wave after wave against the Croatian goal. "Use your left foot, you fool!", "Jesus, Maria, I though he'd scored!", "Ref are you blind?!" interspersed with fruitier Polish exclamations. Many of the men wore floppy red hats adorned with the Polish white eagle. Overwhelmingly they were drinking their Okocim and Tyskie beers direct from bottles. Saves the barmaid's time in washing up glasses, I thought, as I watched the rosy-cheeked young lady with a metal stud in her nose swan around the tables collecting empty bottles. And it would protect her manicured finger nails as well.

I feared a repeat of the cry of rage with which Poles poured out of this and other Polish pubs in West London at the tail end of the previous match with Austria. Poles had been whooping it up with a goal in hand, dreaming of their progress to the next round when, suddenly, in the last 2 minutes of the game, a fowl was awarded against Poland by English referee

Howard Webb. The penalty shot ended in the net, Poland was left with a useless draw and overnight Webb became the most hated man in Polish London. Somehow nobody was blaming the Polish full back for pulling his opponent's shirt in the penalty box. "Hey, in English club football it happens all the time," Mirek, one young Polish "expert", told me.

However this night the Croatia game petered out along with all Polish hopes of survival. No rage here this time. Basically they had come for a funeral, and they got one. They clapped politely when the match was over and walked back out into the street, quiet as lambs, their dreams long shattered, the reality of their every day chores and stress stretching ahead of them long into a distant and unknown future. Until the next Euro finals in four years' time in fact, and those would be held in Poland.

Ealing Gazette - 4th July 2008

New Monument in Ravenscourt Park

Joggers and picnickers in Ravenscourt Park may have noticed a strange new rectangular granite slab emerging like an alien meteorite from the grass near the ornamental lake. It possesses a kind of savage beauty, with its grey coloured surface and black inscription topped by the "Solidarnosc" logo in vivid red. Older visitors to the park may well remember this logo from the 1980s, once almost as iconic a symbol in England as McDonalds. Solidarnosc (or simply Solidarity) represented the mass trade union and social movement in Poland which shook the old Communist regime to the core. Despite brutal suppression under the jackboot of martial law, Solidarity emerged triumphantly in the end as it formed the first democratic government in post-war Central Europe. Without Solidarity the Berlin Wall would still be standing. The democratic united Europe of today owes a great debt to Solidarity and its peaceful struggle.

The new memorial celebrates the work of Giles Hart, a British BT engineer and a veteran campaigner against all forms of tyranny, slavery and torture, who emerged as the Chairman of the Polish Solidarity Campaign in Britain and from his office at the Polish Centre (POSK), overlooking Ravenscourt Park, organised a very effective campaign of support for the Solidarity movement. He also set up the Polish Refugees Rights Group which still operates successfully in Hammersmith today in the form of the East European Advice Centre. Giles was personally thanked by the legendary Solidarity leader Lech Walesa when the latter visited Ealing Town Hall in 1989 just after Poland recovered its freedom. Tragically Giles Hart died in the bombed bus at Tavistock Square in July 2005, a victim of another violent tyranny of the kind with which he had struggled all his life.

The unveiling of the memorial by the Polish Ambassador and the new young Mayor of Hammersmith and Fulham, Councillor Andrew Johnson, took place on July 5th in the presence of the new Chairman of the Solidarity Union, Janusz Sniadek, who had travelled in especially from the Solidarity

HQ in Gdansk in Poland. Other guests included the closest family and friends of Giles, Polish WWII veterans, local MPs and councillors, British trade unionists and a wide cross-section of donors, both Polish and British. His friend Karen Blick gave an eloquent personal tribute. A reception followed in POSK and there was a display of Solidarity memorabilia and Giles' personal archives in the POSK foyer.

In the minute's silence for the victims of the July bombings and afterwards, as the head of the organising committee droned on with a list of "thank yous" exceeding the longest Oscar acceptance speech, the thoughts of participants drifted to those uplifting days when Solidarity marched its millions in defiance of Soviet oppressors, while the free world looked on in unbelieving admiration. Friends remembered Giles as the determined and obstinate but self-effacing leader of PSC, preaching Solidarity's optimistic message of achieving freedom through a peaceful confrontation with tyranny. As the memorial was unveiled all eyes rested finally on the quotation from Mahatma Gandhi inscribed in Polish and English on the memorial, "Be the change you want to see in this world." The struggle for Giles' values should continue anew in each of us.

Ealing Gazette – July 25th 2008

It's just not cricket

I sat idly in the sunshine on the bench outside the Drayton Manor School pavilion in Greenford with a can of beer in my hand as my gaze wandered slowly over the white clad figures scattered in attentive poses around the field. It was the perfect warm English Sunday. It was all there - a cricket match, the sound of leather on willow and dark clouds on the near horizon boding a sudden rainfall and a break in the game.

In fact this was no ordinary game. It was the Tories' Ealing Eleven headed by Council Leader Jason Stacey against the local Labour team headed by MP Steve Pound. Despite their inevitable hostile rivalry across the Council chamber and in newspaper columns, here they had the chance to channel their enmity away from the ritualistic bombast and sound bite of political debate to the equally ritualistic rulebook of the county cricket manual. The prize was the Mayor's Cup brought during a fleeting visit by the Mayor of Ealing. Who said that politics and sport do not mix?

Yet as I watched the play, followed by an unexpected victory for the Comrades ("Gordon Brown will be proud of us," beamed Steve Pound accepting the cup from be-hatted umpire Anthony Young, "a Labour victory at last!"), I noticed one unique element to this game. Each side had a Polish player. On the Conservative side, ever open to equal opportunities, there was cheery Ealing Common Councillor Joanna Dabrowska, sporting a sexy pair of shin pads, and on the other - my own long-haired son, Sandro, who was one of the opening batsmen. And this was odd. Because Poles do not normally play cricket.

I have often tried to explain the rules of cricket with its strange vocabulary and gestures to bewildered Poles. I explain that cricket has been the great social leveller ever since the eighteenth century when the squire could be bowled out by his own gardener. I point out that along with the Queen and the English language, cricket is the third mysterious force that binds the Commonwealth. It is the great mystical ceremony played religiously every Sunday during summer on the village green or on TV sets for the interminable Test matches which gives the agnostic Englishman the only opportunity to experience a sense of eternity. I say all this and the Poles still shake their heads in disbelief.

So it's like "palant"? they ask politely. Well, not really. The Polish game of "palant" is the equivalent of the children's game – rounders. Polish and German settlers first introduced "palant" to America in the XIXth century and it evolved into, (wait for it!) American baseball. Today "palant" can still be played in dusty playgrounds at Polish summer camps. It is certainly not so hidebound by tradition and the scholarship of "Wisden". In fact, it is held in such little regard that in Polish the term "palant" is also the word for a "idiot". By contrast in England there can be no worse words of criticism than the understated phrase "it's just not cricket".

Brits have to understand that for Poles cricket is simply a boring enigma. Poles have to understand that in England cricket is simply the equivalent of civilisation as we know it.

Ealing Gazette – August 29th 2008

Concert at Wembley Arena

Can you imagine 13,000 delirious homesick young Poles jigging, screaming and dancing in a frenzy of rock music within the cavernous embrace of the Wembley Arena? Believe me, it is an awesome sight.

In fact the actual audience was much bigger as the concert was watched by satellite link up with Polish TV so hundreds of thousands of Polish fans both in Poland itself and in other countries, stretching from the Atlantic to the Urals, where Poles work and live, watched it too.

However for the Wembley audience proper there was a ten hour music-fest with the latest and best performers of the Polish music world ranging from the suggestive romantic Natalia Kukulska ("You're so tender disco lover, sexi flexi undercover") to the heavier deafening sound of Lady Pank's "Less than Zero". Not only that. There was also an opportunity for a substantial social get-together and a chance to win lottery prizes in the form of new cars, scooters and laptops.

The audience was in a buzz and ready to party right from the start. This surprised performers like the brooding dark-haired Kayah who had expected that an audience would need stoking up as it does in the more inhibited Polish provinces. Here the singer could let rip with "Testosterone" and the audience response was immediately electric. Wilki ("The Wolves") barely had to say the name "Bashka" and the ecstatic audience belted out the catchphrases. Doda, the Polish Britney Spears (but without the trauma), had but to make her customary slinky entrance, dressed as Catwoman, and the roof of the Arena nearly blew off. The Bajm group could not continue their performance till their blonde singer had satisfied their fans' craving for "Water in the Desert".

The simple truth is that their 4 year presence in Britain and their attendance at numerous British concerts has made the London Poles more adventurous, more brazen, more demanding than their counterparts on the Vistula. Even the VIPs, which included the Polish Foreign Minister Radek Sikorski and the wife of former President Kwasniewski, had no compunction in standing in their seats and joining in the rhythm, as the larger audience cavorted and hugged below.

The PKO Bank Polski, the popular savings bank which had opened their first branch in London last year, were the hosts and sponsors of this magical event. Apparently it was the largest ever concert of Polish music outside Poland. It gave the hard-working youngsters an exhilarating taste of home as well as an opportunity to meet with fellow countrymen. As they trudged their way home emotionally exhausted, they had nurtured in their collective memory that extra spark that could make their daytime work routine more bearable in the weeks to come. It also whet their appetites for the next concert.

Ealing Gazette – September 26th 2008

Annex 1

Polish community in the UK presented by Wiktor Moszczynski, Spokesman, Federation of Poles in Gr. Britain, 12th March 2008 Report to All ParliamentaryCommittee on Poland

I propose to say a few words about the Polish community who form the bulk of the so-called A8 nationals who have come to this country in large numbers since 2004. I am not really in a position to talk about the other nationals – Lithuanians, Estonians, Latvians, Czechs, Hungarians, Slovaks and Slovenes, except to say that their experience mirrors that of the Poles who have come here, to a smaller degree. Poles form 60% of the total intake if these new arrivals from the 8 accession states from Central (not Eastern) Europe that joined the European Union in 2004. I also wish to stress that the citizens from these states who come to the UK tend to see themselves as EU citizens or EU workers with their families, rather than as migrants.

So how many Poles are there in the UK? There are more solid facts in the study of Astrology than in the study of Polish Demographics in the UK. Government statistics seem to be based on four major sources of information about the number of Poles in the UK. The first two are the Labour Force Survey and the International Passenger Surveys. Both are flawed because they are based on random samples and not on solid total figures, though undoubtedly the former survey does give an interesting sociological glimpse about possible trends in the Polish community in Britain. The latter survey is of little use as it fails to record anything except arrivals through the major London airports and Channel Tunnel and takes little consideration of arrivals and departures from provincial airports. In any case a border control system that records people entering the country but not leaving it leaves a much skewed picture of immigration in this country which is exploited by organizations like Migration Watch UK and the British National Party.

The third source is the Worker Registration Scheme which was introduced in 2004 in order to regulate A8 citizens seeking to work here. It required everyone seeking employment to register at a cost of £50 (now £90), and then to register again (free of charge) every time they change jobs. The act of regulation was supposed to ensure that new A8 workers would also be paying taxes and national insurance. It was seen as a useful tool at the beginning, both for the Government which was seen to act responsibly in the face of a large influx of new workers (then estimated at about 13,000 new arrivals every year), and for new arrivals to help accommodate them to settlement and to legal employment in the UK, which would also assure them immediately of rights to child benefit and to use of the health service. After one year, if they should lose their jobs, they would be eligible for other subsidies such as jobseekers allowance. According to WRS statistics administered by the Home Office a total of 327,538 Poles registered for work between May 2004 and December 2006. A lower figure, some 150,000 Poles registered in 2007, of which 38,000 in the last quarter. On February 16th 2008 "The Times" noted this drop, got very excited and announced that the Poles were leaving the UK.

This information was misleading because of the innate flaws of the WRS. The truth is the WRS is expensive and bureaucratic and it never covered the many thousands of Poles who declared themselves to be self-employed. Furthermore few Poles bothered to record changes in employment after one year. When newly arrived Poles or formerly self-employed Poles sought to register after 2006, Home Office advice was not to bother as registration was no longer compulsory. Later these Poles found that failing to register made them ineligible to all benefits except child benefit. The regional statistics based on WRS also proved highly unreliable, noting, for instance low figures in Northern Ireland and the Scottish Highlands, where they were high and showing Camden and Westminster as the London boroughs with the largest population of Poles, when all other evidence showed that the largest concentrations were in Ealing, Brent and Haringey. They showed that the largest group of Poles worked in administration, business and management, which sounds optimistic until you realize that this covers all those hired as temps through cheap recruitment agencies.

We have found the fourth statistical source, the National Insurance Registration figures, to be the most reliable source of information on Poles in this country, though imperfections remain. We trust the NI figures both at national and local level because they correlate with other important local statistics such as the number of children speaking Polish, numbers of Polish births and numbers of Polish citizens on the electoral register. Between 2001 and 2006 - 333,000 Poles had been registered for National Insurance. In the year 2006/2007 a further 223,000 were registered making a total of 556.000. Please note that that last year showed an actual increase, not a decrease in registration, on the previous year. So much for "The Times" analysis.

However it is generally accepted that there are more Poles who have come here and have not registered for work but are working nonetheless. Many of these are seasonal. The total Polish Embassy estimate last year was 600,000 with more during the summer season. Statistics from Poland indicate that perhaps up to a million have come here but not necessarily stayed, or may have come more than once in a year. Let us also not forget 57,000 British residents recorded as being of Polish origin in the 2001 Census, plus a further 100,000 or so second and third generation Poles living in this country. The best solution is to say there are 800,000 Poles in the UK including the older indigenous Polish population.

A useful guide to their geographical distribution throughout the UK is to record which constituencies had more than 1000 new Poles registered for National Insurance in the last year. Here is the list: Acton and Shepherds Bush, Bedford, Birmingham Ladywood, Birmingham Perry Bar, Boston & Skegness, Brent East, Brent South, Brentford and Isleworth, Crewe and Nantwich, Doncaster Central, Hackney North, Hornsey & Wood Green, Leeds Central, Leicester West, Mitcham & Morden, Northampton

South, Nottingham East, Oxford East, Peterborough, Salford, Southall, Southampton Test, Streatham, Walthamstow, West Ham, Aberdeen North, Edinburgh East, Glasgow Central and Inverness & Nairn. Also 5 constituencies recorded more than 2000 new NI registered Poles: Ealing North, Luton South, Slough, Tottenham and Edinburgh North & Leith. 8900 Poles were also registered in Northern Ireland last year.

According to the DWP, one third of the Poles who came before 2006 are employed in administration business and management, 22% in hospitality and catering, 10% in agriculture, 8% in manufacturing, 6% in the health service, 5% in food processing, just under 5% in the retail trade and the same again in the construction industry. There is therefore a wider variety than the Polish plumber and builder. Their input into agriculture has been particularly appreciated in Scotland and rural areas like Wales and Lincolnshire where they have effectively rescued Britain's fresh food production. Their work ethic is much admired by their employers and they are often seen to take jobs that the indigenous population have failed to take up. According to the IOD, out of 500 employers surveyed by them 61% say they hire Poles because of their superior skills and only 16% because they were cheaper. 32% of this workforce has had a university education; more than 90% are less than 40 years old.

And yet according to other surveys conducted in 2006, some 80% were employed initially in the region of £4.50 and £5.99 per hour, so just below and above the national minimum wage. This is almost certainly changed as more and more Poles are making promising careers in areas such as accountancy, banking and responsible jobs in industry and administration but a lot are kept in low pay jobs and often work illegal hours and in dangerous forms of employment without adequate insurance for injuries. Driven here by the then 19% unemployment rate in Poland and by an average monthly wage of £800 a month, they found even these low paid jobs attractive especially if they economized by staying in tied accommodation or in low quality multi-occupational housing with hot bedding and some 3 to a room. Many of those with a poor knowledge of English were exploited both by English employers and Polish middlemen who often cheated them of their hard-earned money. The action of trades unions in seeking to recruit Polish workers, in fighting for better pay and working conditions for them has been an invaluable help, as has the tightening up of the licensing of gang masters in agriculture and the food industry. Unfortunately workers in the hospitality and construction industries do not have the same protection and remain exposed to unregistered recruitment agencies.

According to surveys conducted by the University of Surrey in 2006, some 16% of those who came here had a specific short term aim to earn enough to buy property or invest in a business in Poland. 20% are here to earn money seasonally and rarely stay more than 6 months at a time though they are ready to return the following year, 22% were ready to stay here long term, perhaps permanently, and some 42% had simply no definite plan about their future. Because of this it has been particularly difficult to predict the future trends or to invest in more permanent institutions. Poles remain highly mobile. Cheap coach journeys and economy flights from provincial airports ensure that 80% of them travel back and forth between Poland and UK at least once (and often several times) a year, and 70% retain regular contact with families by phone, mobile and money transfer. For this reason any statistics based on border crossings are meaningless in measuring the number of Poles in UK.

The same survey showed that 72% come from rural backgrounds or from small provincial towns in Poland and these are the people least likely to have a knowledge of English, least likely to know their rights as employees and tenants and least aware of how to adapt to a multiethnic society. About 38% questioned for instance showed a racist attitude to intermarriage, although a majority were ready to conform to British standards. Those with young families found it much easier to adapt as their children went to school and learned about the British way of life, though this can still remain a problem with older Polish teenagers in secondary schools in inner urban areas who often resent being brought to the UK and separated from their friends in Poland by their parents.

Much of this would improve with time but there is also a discernible rise in hate crimes against Poles particularly outside the large cities. In rural communities the Polish minorities are highly visible. Poles are not just the victims of crime. Newspapers articles and the police have referred to the large number of crimes committed by Poles in the UK, more than 7000 arrestable offences in 2007. Overwhelmingly these are for lesser crimes and the possibility of a Polish citizen being arrested in the UK is statistically 3 times less likely than it would be for an ordinary resident in the UK. A particular problem is the high proportion of motoring offences, especially drink-driving. Polonophobic sentiments continue to fester, particularly among British residents with a low level of economic or social achievement, and this sentiment is sustained by sensational headlines in newspapers like the "Daily Mail".

Local police forces, local authorities and health trusts are often overwhelmed by the need for Polish translators, Polish advice centres and places at day schools. There were 7179 children registered in London local authority schools alone last year with Polish as a first language. There is a tug of war between local authorities and the central government based again on a different interpretation of statistics. The recent introduction by the Government of Exceptional Circumstances Grants and the New Arrivals Excellence Programme to help local authorities with a high number of foreign pupils is to be welcomed.

A further complication for the local health trusts is the difficulty for Poles to register with local health clinics and GPs because of a lack of utility bills and then this causes them to overutilize the A&E departments of local hospitals for the slightest medical problem.

According to the National Bank of Poland about £4bn are sent each year by Polish workers in the UK to their families at home. However according to the National Institute of Economic and Social Research the Polish workforce contributed £12 billion to the British economy in the years 2004 to 2006. So both economies have gained from their presence. According to Piotr Grzeszkiewicz, director of recruitment agency Sara-Int, the Polish workforce contributes about £1.9 billion a year to the British exchequer in income tax and national insurance and this does not include council tax.

While Poles with families can claim child benefit (some £21 million), regardless of whether their children are in the UK or Poland, only 3% of the Polish workforce are eligible for out of work subsidies like the Job Seekers Allowance after working here for more than a year and then being made redundant.

Many of these Poles came to the UK because of the vibrant economy and the opportunities offered by the British Government in its courageous decision in 2004 to open the British labour market to the A8 countries. But an added attraction was a historic wartime link between Poland and the UK reinforced by the presence of a large Polish community in this country since the end of the Second World War. This older community saw themselves initially as temporary political exiles but once it had accustomed itself to the fact it would not returning to a free independent Poland, it sought to settle permanently in Britain in the spirit of economic integration but without necessarily cultural assimilation. It was enriched by new waves of Polish immigrants in the 1950s and 1980s. Over the decades, the Polish diaspora became a model for integration of other communities into the UK. The new Polish arrivals in this decade appeared to almost swamp the older community and the two initially lived totally separate lives but the presence of the older settlers is making it much easier for the new Polish arrivals to adapt themselves slowly to British life.

There is a vibrant Polish Catholic Mission in England and Wales, independent of the British Roman Catholic hierarchy. It administers over 134 parishes, but in fact mass can be heard every week in at least 224 places of worship around England and Wales. The Polish church in Ealing sees an average 5000 Polish worshippers attending one of eight masses each Sunday. The Polish Catholic Mission in Scotland has 18 parishes. Many of these Polish churches also have charity volunteers who give advice to the homeless, drug addicts, alcoholics and their families.

The Federation of Poles in Great Britain is an umbrella organization for the traditional Polish secular organizations in the UK and has over 80 member organizations, of which nearly 10 are from the new community. There are 74 Polish Saturday schools teaching the Polish language and customs from nursery age to A level courses. The largest such school in Ealing has around 600 pupils. There are two Polish universities in London.

There is a Polish Daily which has been published in London since 1941 and 5 weekly magazines some with a print run of over 25,000 distributed throughout all the major Polish centres. There are 3 radio stations and an internet TV station now linked to the Sky channel. All of these play a major role in seeking to integrate the new Poles into British society and British economy while sustaining interest in Polish culture, traditions and news from the homeland. Apart from the churches and media there is a lot of useful advice from Polish speaking staff in free advice centres subsidized by both Polish and UK funding, although some private firms exploit the unwary charging high prices for simple translations and photocopying. The Polish Consulate used to be overwhelmed with people seeking help but they are coping better now and are opening a branch in Manchester.

There are several hundred Polish firms in the construction, production and retail industries as well as some 100,000 self-employed Poles in various cottage industries. Polish food, fresh as well as tinned, is available in thousands of outlets throughout the country from Indian shops, Polish delicatessens through to the big supermarkets. High street banks vie for Polish business and make it possible for Central Europeans to open a bank account without the need for utility bills. There is a visible Polish presence on the streets of Britain, in places of entertainment and on public transport.

Certainly growth in the Polish economy and a change in the exchange rate of the zloty to the pound (from 7.2 per £ in 2004 to 4.83 per £ this month) have contributed to a slow down in the arrivals of Poles in the UK by the end of last year. Some 22,000 have gone back permanently. Many have returned because they had achieved their short term goals and there are more opportunities in Poland constructing Stadiums and roads for the 2012 UEFA championships. Large cities like Warsaw, Wroclaw and Gdansk are urging Poles with their newly acquired skills to return ("But not all at once," said the Deputy Mayor of Gdansk in a TV interview in December). Other EU countries are now opening their labour markets to the Poles as well. The election results in October last year, leading to the collapse of the eccentric Kaczynski government have also removed an important psychological barrier to Poles returning but the unresolved issue of double taxation on earnings in the UK and suspended social benefits in Poland after a 2 year absence will remain a barrier for many homesick Poles until they are resolved.

There is no doubt that the peak of Polish visitors has been passed but we do not expect a mass migration of Poles out of the UK. We estimate that in 5 years time some 60% of those Poles who settled here will not have left, especially those with good employment prospects or with children in English schools. Probably about 20% will remain here permanently but in an age of increasing migration this will become less and less noticeable and all EU citizens should feel at home wherever they are in the European Union.

Nevertheless, in view of some of the problems that I have mentioned, I believe that there is a need for a coordinated approach between the Department of Communities and Local Government, the Department of Work and Pensions and the Home Office to ensure that

1/ Arrival figures no longer become a measure of migration for EU citizens unless they are balanced with departure figures

2/ An accurate nationwide summary is drawn up of all local government statistics on Polish children in schools, Poles on electoral registers, records on local employment, local births and deaths, to be published by the Office of National Statistics

3/ An interim National Census should be held every 5 years

4/ There should be a permanent police unit monitoring crime statistics on Poles as victims and perpetrators

5/ Free lessons in the English language and UK civics for all Polish citizens offered through their places of employment or in local community centres

6/ Greater participation by the Polish community representatives in the work of the Equalities and Human Rights Commission, Migration Impact Forum and all government studies reviewing the role of foreign nationals, as in the NHS

7/ Easier access for Poles to register with GP surgeries

8/ Scaling down or even the suspension of the Worker Registration Scheme for A8 nationals

9/ Licensing of Gangmaster Agencies should be extended to the construction and hospitality industries

10/ Definition of Racism should be legally extended to discrimination on grounds of nationality or ethnic origin and be a recognized as a disciplinary offence for public employees

Annex 2 -

Federation of Poles: online Daily Mail article

Older readers of the Daily Mail will be aware that here has been a sizeable Polish community in this country since World War Two when Polish forces fought alongside British servicemen against the Nazi threat. Since then, an estimated one million Polish citizens have arrived in the UK after European Union expansion in 2004, mostly to work. They have made a significant contribution to both the Polish and British economies. According to the National Bank of Poland, about £4 billion is sent each year by Polish workers in the UK to their families at home. However – according to the National Institute of Economic and Social Research – the Polish workforce alone has contributed £12 billion to the British economy between 2004 and 2006.

We have all heard about the cheap Polish plumbers and seen the smiling Polish waitresses and shop assistants. Poles have helped to revive British agriculture (especially in Scotland, Wales and Lincolnshire) and to boost, until earlier this year, the recent house-building boom in this country. Unfortunately many were exploited as they struggled to obtain the legal minimum wage and basic employment rights. At the other end of the economic scale, thousands of entrepreneurs have now set up their own businesses, while others can be found in responsible positions in the NHS, social services, accountancy and banking.

We have evidence that the Polish workforce contributes about £1.9 billion a year to the British exchequer in income tax and national insurance, not including council tax. Poles are integrating well into the British way of life, especially if they are setting up families here. Of course we are aware that their presence has impacted considerably on the resources of local councils, schools and health trusts, but much of this is covered by tax contributions.

The Federation of Poles in Great Britain has been concerned about newspaper coverage which has sought to emphasise negative aspects of the

Polish presence in the UK. In our view, the worst examples linked Poles with words and phrases like "feckless", "chancers", "race riots", "swamp the NHS", "fears for schools", "cut-price treatment", "push British graduates to back of the jobs queue", "killers, drug smugglers and rapists". We consider that this has made Poles living in the UK feel vulnerable and persecuted.

Some might argue that these robust headlines were aimed more at the British Government, its immigration policy and at the European Union. Fair enough. This implies therefore that Poles came into the firing line not because they were Poles but because they were the most visible symbol of those government policies that the Daily Mail has criticised. The Federation remains critical however of the lack of reliable national and local government statistics on the number and impact of Poles in this country.

We maintain that Poles have felt humiliated by the coverage and are vulnerable to numerous acts of overt hostility and even violence which they have experienced from a vociferous minority of UK citizens. There have been hundreds of cases of hate crime against Poles in this country recorded in the last 2 years, some leading to death or permanent injury, and we would not want these incidents to be encouraged by potentially inflammatory newspaper stories or headlines.

In some ways the heat is off now. A good proportion of Poles have either already returned or are planning to do so soon as the Polish economy improves and the Polish currency almost doubles in value against sterling. There is now more concern in the press and economic circles about the impact of their departure rather than of their arrival. Nevertheless a significant number are here and will continue to be here for some years. The need for sensitive reporting and sensitive headlines remains.

Wiktor Moszczynski,
Press Spokesman,
Federation of Poles in Great Britain 5th August 2008

Annex 3

Speech at Reception with Mayor of London at City Hall - 25th July 2007

Mr Mayor, Councillors, Ladies and Gentlemen and friends,

The Chairman and Vice-Chairman of the Federation of Poles both apologize for not being able to attend today and have asked me to make comments on their behalf and on behalf of the Federation of Poles in GB. The Federation is the umbrella group which includes the main secular Polish organizations in this country (such as the Polish Social and Cultural Centre, the Polish Education Society and the Ex-Combatants Association) and is often viewed as the voice of the Polish community.

The Polish community in this country, and especially in London, is actually a hybrid including many elderly Poles who remained as war veterans and political exiles after WWII, as well as their children and grandchildren, and also the later arrivals throughout the sixties, seventies and eighties. They have left their mark on the London landscape: the Sikorski Institute in Kensington, the Polish Library in Hammersmith, the Polish War Memorial in Northolt, the Sikorski statue in Portland Place and numerous Polish churches. They are often well settled now and could be a model of how a minority can be integrated into British society without losing its cultural identity.

In the last 6 years we have seen new arrivals in this country, overwhelmingly young and single, often well educated, encouraged by the Government's generous decision to allow new EU citizens access to filling the skills shortage in the UK labour market. This has largely paid off as the CEBR estimate that Poles contribute £4bn per year to the British economy, leaving aside income from taxes. At least one third of that would benefit the London economy.

Figures vary but we estimate that there are at least 150,000 Poles within the Greater London area of whom, according to surveys, some 50% are now likely to stay longer The fact that there are some 55,000

Polish electors in London (which is nearly half the electorate of a London Borough like Richmond), 8000 Polish-speaking children in London state schools, nearly 70,000 paying national insurance and nearly 60,000 on the increasingly unpopular Worker Registration Scheme are further evidence that many are considering a long term stay. The majority of these would have prospered sufficiently to feel they can lay down roots here.

Consequently a Polish archipelago is appearing all over London, not only in traditional Polish areas like Ealing, Hammersmith, Brent and Wandsworth but in new areas where there was no established Polish organization, such as in Haringey, Barnet, Lambeth, Southwark and Newham. Within these scattered Polish enclaves we see a mushrooming of Polish delicatessens, as well as Indian shops and eventually the big supermarket giants selling Polish food. We have 12 Polish Saturday schools, five weeklies, one daily and 3 radio stations, while Polish Catholic churches have become the envy of their other religious neighbours with their packed church congregations lustily singing Polish hymns. Polish rock concerts take place regularly in various London town halls. There are now Polish professionals in the NHS, in accountancy and in the City of London; the high street banks are in sharp competition for the so-called Polish pound and few London eating establishments are without at least one Polish waitress.

On the flipside, we recognize that there are undoubted social strains emanating from the increased Polish presence here. They arise from increasing sharper competition in the job market and the growing need for local government and health services to find the extra resources for London schools, health clinics, housing trusts, police and social services. May we remind you that Polish workers make a substantial contribution towards those costs with their council taxes but this does not alleviate the problem entirely. The return of free English language lessons and courses on the British way of life is a necessity in order to aid in the integration process.

There is also a minority, not an insignificant one and certainly a very visible one, but still a minority, who have failed to make a success of their stay. Often without language skills, unable to adapt to London's bracing market economy and high cost of living, they live in squalor in multi-occupational houses sometimes seven to a room, or even on the streets, have low paid jobs, even below the minimum wage, and much of the time they are without a job at all. Their presence requires compassionate but resolute coordinated solutions, both by British authorities (national and local), charitable institutions, Polish organizations in this country and in Poland.

Though the London public and the national media reacted initially to this new Polish presence with generosity of spirit, praising Polish plumbers and bar staff, we know that some of these social problems do cause a strain and there have been instances of discrimination and even violence of a racial nature towards Poles. These have been egged on by extremist organizations and by irresponsible media sensationalism often fuelled by the wish to settle political scores with the British government or the European Union. We hope that you will monitor these examples along with us in the same spirit as you would monitor discrimination towards any other kind of minority.

Both the older community and the new are now Londoners. We are all part of the social fabric of this splendid capital city. We want good schools, good hospitals, good public transport like every other Londoner. We enjoy the cultural splendours and endure the vicissitudes of commuter travel and the fear of crime like every other Londoner. During the July 7th bombing outrage 3 young Polish women were killed, the largest contingent of foreign nationals among the victims. We are here for the good and the bad times; more part of the solution than part of the problem.

Mr Mayor, we know and appreciate your concern over inclusiveness of London's many and varied minorities. We for our part do not want to live in a Polish ghetto. We are anxious that the new Polish intake which seeks to settle here can find increasing prosperity for themselves in a harmonious environment.

We thank you for your invitation and look forward to future cooperation and understanding between the Polish communities in London and the Greater London Authority.

Thank you.

Annex 4

House of Lords Report on Impact of Immigration

Their Lordships have spoken. The 82 page report covers all kinds of immigrants, from the New Commonwealth and the New Europe. Searching through this morass of graphs and witness statements, I have failed to find any recognition of the current status of the ever visible Polish workers within the British society and the British economy.

Needless to say that out of those 70 witnesses, not one was a Pole or a Central European. There was not a single expert witness from abroad or from the immigrant communities, many of whom have eminent scholars in the field of economics and sociology who could have contributed. Not for the first time Poles experience a déjà vu of the "Yalta syndrome": Polish issues are discussed without any Polish input.

Some of the report conclusions were pretty obvious. The Federation of Poles in Great Britain has been badgering ministers and MPs constantly about the abysmal lack of reliable statistics, the resentment felt by those on low incomes or unemployed at the new influx of hard-working Poles, the ruthless exploitation of some of the immigrant workers, the lack of school place provision for the families of new workers at the local level, the need to intensify the ESOL programme for free English lessons. While we supported the Government's controversial decision in 2004 to allow citizens of the new EU states to work in Britain, we were concerned at the lack of foresight over the social problems that would inevitably accompany such a large influx. Only 13,000 would come every year, said the Government. One of the funniest pages in the report (which, all in all, was no barrel of laughs) was the appendix to the report which recounted how German social scientists advising the government got this prediction so terribly wrong.

The House of Lords Report acknowledged that immigrants contributed some £6bn into the British economy but then made the astounding statement that this "was irrelevant". Since when has GDP been irrelevant? It is always an important factor in the measure of any economy. Instead their Lordships stated that this increase should be measured on income per head of each indigenous resident and on that basis they conclude that the benefits for these residents "were small". The main beneficiaries, the report claims, are large scale employers and the immigrants themselves; the losers those on low incomes and other national minorities.

The Little Englanders who have consistently opposed immigration right through the last decades took no time to say "I told you so!" and inevitably the number of "hate crimes" against Poles in the rural areas will increase as a result. One could see similar outbursts of rage when earlier immigration of Flemmings in the XIVth century and Huguenots in the XVIIth century enriched the English economy but left a large proportion of the population feeling resentful and destitute. Similar reactions occurred with the advent of industrialization and when the labour market was opened increasingly to women. These understandable pockets of resentment occur because the economic gains of society have never been evenly distributed amongst the population and because the welfare benefits system does not encourage many of the indigenous residents to seek work. Hardly the fault of the Poles!

The 600,000 or so Poles who have come here in the last 5 years definitely came to work. True, many of their children go to school, they are treated by the NHS, they receive child benefit but only 3% are eligible for other subsidies. There is a true extra burden on local health authorities and police associations. Many of these social costs however are covered by their £1.9 billion a year contribution to the British exchequer in income tax and national insurance and that figure does not include their contribution to Council tax.

Their presence has been hugely popular among the middle classes who needed plumbers and nannies, blessed (literally) by the newly dominant Roman Catholic Church, and welcomed by the food and construction industries, local public transport and by Scottish agriculture which they have saved from extinction. Now recruiting sergeants from the British Army want them too. Their work ethic has been praised by employers, customers and fellow workers alike though it is resented by those who feel that the crowded labour market for the unskilled and lowly paid is no longer a level playing field.

And what is the alternative? Stories that many Poles may be returning to a more prosperous Poland are a little exaggerated but they have been cheered by the malcontents and raised panic amongst employers particularly in the rural industries. The "Daily Mail" which has been belabouring Poles consistently for their presence is now calling them "deserters" for threatening to leave. I could find nothing in the House of Lords Report that answered this question.

Wiktor Moszczynski
Published in "Daily Telegraph" - 3rd April 2008 .

Annex 5

100 MOST INFLUENTIAL RESIDENTS OF POLISH ORIGIN IN THE HISTORY AND LIFE OF GREAT BRITAIN

Wladyslaw Anders, general, charismatic WWII commander of Second Polish Corps
Anton Antonowicz, "Daily Mirror" war correspondent
Arkadius, eccentric fashion designer (surname Weremczuk)
Konrad Bartelski, 1980s Olympic skiing champion
Josef Bartosik, Rear-Admiral, Ass.Chief Naval Staff (Operations) in late Sixties
Andrzej Blonski, architect, built theatres in Milton Keynes and Plymouth
Chris Bobinski "Financial Times" journalist
Jan Bobrowski, design engineer of bridges and stadium (including Arsenal FC)
Mark Borkowski, flamboyant PR consultant
Jacob Bronowski, scientist, TV broadcaster, author of "Ascent of Man"
Stefan Buczacki, authority on gardening, author of "Gardening Dictionary"
Canute, King of England, Denmark & Norway, son of Sweyn and Swietoslawa
Charles Edward Stuart ("Bonnie Prince Charlie"), the Young Pretender
Jan Ciechanowski, historian and academic
Lindka Cierach, dress designer to the royal family
Joseph Conrad, maritime novelist, author of "Lord Jim" and "Nostromo"
Isaac Deutscher, historian and Marxist theoretician, biographer of Stalin and Trotsky
Kazimierz Deyna, centre forward, Manchester City FC in the 1970s

K J Drewienkiewicz, major-general, Commander of British Mission in Kosovo
Jerzy Dudek, goalkeeper for Liverpool FC
Olenka Frenkiel, TV investigative journalist and newsreader
Stanislaw Frenkiel, sensuous painter and illustrator
Jozef Garlinski, wartime historian, author of "Fighting Auschwitz"
Sir John Gielgud, classic Shakespearean actor and film actor
Stanislaw Gomulka, academic, LSE professor of economics
Henryk Gotlib, post-war landscape painter, draughtsman, art historian
Oskar Halecki, post-war historian, books on Europe, biographer of Pius XII
Barbara Hamilton-Kaczmarowska, portrait painter
Samuel Hartlib, XVII century education reformer, adviser to Oliver Cromwell
Barbara Hulanicki, founder of "Biba" department store, style icon of Swinging Sixties
Felix Janiewicz, early XIXth C composer, conductor of London Philharmonic Orchestra
Waldemar Januszczak, art critic of "The Guardian" and "The Times", TV broadcaster
Joanna Kanska, TV actress, "A Very Peculiar Practice", "Lovejoy", "Rumpole"
Jacek Kasprzyk, musician, classical conductor
Maria Kempinska, founder of the Jongleur Comedy Club
Leszek Kolakowski, philosopher and Oxford academic
George Kolankiewicz, sociologist, broadcaster, professor at London University
Stanislaw Kopanski, general, commander Polish Carpathian Brigade at Tobruk
Anna Korwin, TV & theatre actress, "Forsyte Saga", "East Enders", "Callas"
Adam Kossowski, sculptor, ecclesiastical mural designer
Jan Kott, cultural historian, author of "Shakespeare; Our Contemporary"

Andrzej Krauze, illustrator and "Guardian" caricaturist
Danuta Kruszynska, fashion dress designer (jointly with sister Liliana)
Leopold Labedz, political journalist, editor of "Survey", biographer of A. Solzhenitsyn
Jan Laski, XVIth C. religious reformer, adviser to King Edward VI
Mark Lazarowicz, MP for Edinburgh North & Leith, leader Edinburgh City Council
Rula Lenska, singer, film and TV actress, "Rock Follies", "Take a Letter, Mr Jones"
Daniel Libeskind, architect,Imp. War Museum,Manchester &London GraduateCentr
Jack Lohman, Director of the Museum of London
Denis MacShane MP for Rotherham, current Minister for Europe
Stanislaw Maczek, gen. commander Polish Armoured Division at Falaise and Breda
John Madejski, founder "Autotrade", Chairman Reading FC, hotel developer, philanthropist
Bronislaw Malinowski, pioneer of social anthropology, author "Freedom & Civilization"
Jozef Mazur, physicist, wartime adviser to RAF, introduced fog dispersal at airports
Sir Lewis Namier, XXth century historian, specialist on British XVIII Century politics
Mike Oborski, Liberal Democrat politician, Mayor of Kidderminster
Andrzej Panufnik, composer, musical director Birmingham Symphony Orchestra
Jerzy Peterkiewicz, novelist, literary historian, author of "The Knotted Cord"
Jan Pienkowski, illustrator, especially of children's books, pioneer of pop-up books
Roman Polanski, film director, "Cul de Sac", "Tess"
Joseph Raca, delicatessen merchant, Chairman of Northampton County Council

Wladyslaw Raczkiewicz, wartime President of Poland in exile in London

Edward Raczynski diplomat, pre-war and wartime Polish Ambassador

Sir Leon Radzinowicz, author of legal textbook "A History of English Law"

Marie Rambert, dance pioneer, founder of "Ballet Rambert"

Joseph Retinger, founder of European Movement, began secret Bildeburg conferences

Jacek Rostowski, professor of economics, UK adviser to post-Communist reformers

Jakub Rostowski, neurologist, post-war Rector of Medical College Edinburgh

Roman Rostowski, colonial administrator, 1st Secretary Mauritius and Seychelles

Sir Joseph Rotblat, nuclear scientist, Nobel Prize winner, initiator of Pugwash debates

Greg Rusedski, tennis player, Wimbledon celebrity

Izabela Scorupco, film actress, Bond girl from "Goldeneye"

Vladek Sheybal, film and TV actor, Bond villain from "From Russia with Love"

Karol Sikora, oncologist, head of WHO Cancer Programme, author of "Fight Cancer"

Wladyslaw Sikorski, general, wartime C-in C and prime minister of Poland

Stanislaw Skalski, wartime fighter pilot ace

Krystyna Skarbek-Granvelle, SOE operator, 1st Brit agent in occupied France

Jerzy Skolimowski, film director ("Moonlighting", "Deep End") and painter

Stanislaw Sosabowski, general, commander of paratroops division at Arnhem

Frank Staff, Conservative politician, Mayor of Wandsworth

Tomasz Starzewski, clothes designer, haute couturier

Mike Strzelecki, Director of Safety & Environment, London Underground

Pawel Strzelecki, XIX century explorer, discovered Mt Kosciusko in Australia

Boleslaw Sulik, TV screenwriter and independent TV producer

Swietoslawa, Xth century princess, wife of Sweyn Forkbeard, mother of Canute

Jan Sykulski, academic, pioneer on electromagnetic research

Henryk Szeryng, violinist

Maria Szymanowska, early XIXc composer, concert pianist, Regency courtier

Feliks Topolski, expressionist painter, wartime illustrator

Tracey Ullman, pop singer, TV and film actress

Andrew Visnievski, theatre producer, director of "The Cherub Company"

Stefan Wagstyl, economic correspondent for Financial Times

Roman Wajda, engineer, founder of POSK (Polish Centre in Hammersmith)

Ernest Wistrich, former MP, Director of the European Movement

Jagna Wright, independent TV film producer, "Forgotten Odyssey" "Another Truth"

Miroslaw Wyszynski, academic,mech. engineer,leader Future Power SystemsGroup

Tadeusz Zablocki-Gwasz, industrialist, philanthropist, journalist

Adam Zamoyski, historian, author of "Holy Madness" and "Last King of Poland"

Marek Zulawski, symbolic painter of Festival of Britain and church murals

Jan Zumbach, wartime RAF ace, post-war merchant advent urer author "Wings of War"

Henryk Zygalski, wartime crypto analyst, invented sheet deciphering Enigma machines

Compiled by Wiktor Moszczyński 2004

Annex 6

EU citizens of Polish origin in London

London Boroughs	Polish-speaking Electors	Polish-speaking School Children	Poles Registered Nat Ins 2002/06
Barking & Dagenham	302	65	430
Barnet	1300	541	3330
Bexley	185	NR	220
Brent	NR	NR	5620
Bromley	601	25	560
Camden	912	101	1240
City of London	16	12	30
Croydon	1066	246	1270
Ealing	6974	1277	9480
Enfield	1376	289	1510
Greenwich	777	76	770
Hackney	1518	275	2920
Hammersmith & Fulham	1785	417	2550
Haringey	3460	552	4940
Harrow	1124	254	1210
Havering	NR	43	230
Hillingdon	883	159	1020
Hounslow	2919	640	4390
Islington	725	125	1580
Kensington & Chelsea	485	129	800
Kingston	624	105	680
Lambeth	1770	194	3550
Lewisham	975	173	1540
Merton	2117	269	2040
Newham	NR	304	2570
Redbridge	NR	118	660
Richmond	NR	141	890
Southwark	1172	127	1810
Sutton	485	74	460
Tower Hamlets	856	95	1900
Waltham Forest	2805	NR	2860
Wandsworth	3211	420	3540
Westminster	701	73	1320
Totals	**41124**	**7329**	**67920**

"NR" means "No Record". 10th June 2007 London

Annex 7

The recorded figures for Polish electors in London are as follows:-

London Borough	Polish Electors 2007	Polish Electors 2008
Barking & Dagenham	302	495
Barnet	1,300	2,712
Bexley	185	287
Brent	NR	NR
Bromley	601	839
Camden	912	901
City of London	16	20
Croydon	1,066	1,655
Ealing	6,974	9,118
Enfield	1,376	2,066
Greenwich	777	1,074
Hackney	1,518	1,792
Hammersmith & Fulham	1,785	1,896
Haringey	3,460	4,267
Harrow	1,124	1,545
Havering	NR	254
Hillingdon	883	1,256
Hounslow	2,919	4,436
Islington	725	969
Kensington & Chelsea	485	522
Kingston	624	941
Lambeth	1,770	2,503
Lewisham	975	1,309
Merton	2,117	3,087
Newham	NR	2,861
Redbridge	NR	NR
Richmond	NR	914
Southwark	1,172	1,524
Sutton	485	701
Tower Hamlets	856	1,269
Waltham Forest	2,805	3,509
Wandsworth	3,211	3,847
Westminster	701	837
Totals	**41,124**	**59,386**

"NR" means "No Record".

Annex 8

SINGLE POLES ARE LEAVING UK, BUT.......
POLISH FAMILIES ARE STAYING
42% more Polish children in London schools

P R E S S R E L E A S E - 28th January 2009

The London-based **Federation of Poles in Great Britain** states today that recent reports by the British press that Polish workers are abandoning the UK *are greatly exaggerated.* The Federation has been in contact with its many branches and organisations, with trade unions and commercial organisations and finds that, despite the credit crunch, Polish working families are increasingly seeking to stay and work in the UK. **Their stay is not necessarily permanent, but it is likely to be more than short term**. It is true that some 200,000 Poles may have departed in the last year, predominantly single Poles or childless couples from rural areas, who had lost their jobs or were looking for better work prospects in countries such as Norway or Holland. It is also true that far fewer new Poles are coming to Britain.

However the Federation estimates that **some 500,000 to 600,000 Poles still remain** here and a large proportion of these are **families with young children**. Our estimates are confirmed by our research on the number of Polish-speaking children in London state schools. After contacting the education departments of all 33 London Boroughs, first in May 2007 and then again in December 2008, we have found a **42.9% increase** in the number of Polish-speaking children over that period. This trend will be reflected to a lesser degree in other parts of the UK. **The detailed London results are in Annex A.**

"The statistics are interesting" says Professor George Kolankiewicz, Rector of the School of Slavonic and East European Studies. "With the

5 year permanent residence status now coming closer for the first wave of post 2004 migrants we are seeing labour migration turning into settlement. All research indicates that they are not likely to seek UK citizenship but will make their future here as Polish citizens under the umbrella of EU legislation. They are generally young, educated and ambitious and will be an injection of human capital for London!"

Mrs Aleksandra Podhoredecka, Chair of the London based Polish Education Society, says "The enclosed statistics indicate clearly that the number of Polish children in schools in London is growing steadily. Judging by recent reports(1) many are doing extremely well once they have mastered English. They will prove to be valuable members of society."

One of the causes of this increase in children is the increasing role in the UK of Polish women deciding on where to settle and bring up their children. They do not want to disrupt their children's education. "Nearly half of all workers registered with the Workers Registration Scheme by 2007 are now women," says migration expert Professor Louise Ryan. "It is apparent that women are active players in the decision-making process." She concludes: "Migrants' planning and decision-making are often implicated in complex family relationships and considerations. While some people migrated alone to support family members in Poland, others decided to reunite their families in London."(2)

For further details please contact Mr Wiktor Moszczynski, press spokesman, Federation of Poles in Great Britain, tel. 07711 912188 or Ms Kasia Zagrodniczek, 0208 748 1203.

Federation website is www.zpwb.org.uk. Federation address, 240 King Street, London W6 0RF

(1)See Rosemary Sales' report 'Polish Pupils in London Schools' published in December 2008 by Middlesex University

2)Louis Ryan, Rosemary Sales, Mary Tilki, Bernadetta Siara (2009) "Family Strategies and Transnational Migration: Recent Polish Migrants in London", "Journal of Ethnic and Migration Studies" 35:1,61-77

ANNEX A

The recorded figures for Polish speaking children in London schools December 2008

London Borough	May-07	Dec-08	+/-
Barking & Dagenham	65	170	+ 162%
Barnet	541	654	+ 21%
Bexley	NR	NR	NR
Brent	205	619	+ 202%
Bromley	25	23	-8%
Camden	101	181	+ 79%
City of London	12	1	-92%
Croydon	246	346	+ 41%
Ealing	1,277	1,876	+ 47%
Enfield	289	406	+ 40%
Greenwich	76	192	+ 153%
Hackney	275	369	+ 34%
Hammersmith & Fulham	417	387	-7%
Haringey	552	671	+ 22%
Harrow	254	401	+ 58%
Havering	43	72	+ 67%
Hillingdon	159	306	+ 92%
Hounslow	640	826	+ 29%
Islington	135	179	+ 33%
Kensington & Chelsea	129	114	- 12%
Kingston	105	122	+ 16%
Lambeth	194	426	+ 120%
Lewisham	173	248	+ 43%
Merton	269	434	+ 61%
Newham	304	481	+ 58%
Redbridge	118	182	+ 54%
Richmond	141	179	+ 27%
Southwark	127	157	+ 24%
Sutton	74	109	+ 47%

Tower Hamlets	95	148	+ 56%
Waltham Forest	324	475	+ 47%
Wandsworth	420	481	+ 15%
Westminster	73	134	+ 84%
Total for all Boroughs	**7,958**	**11,369**	**+ 42.9%**

"NR" means "No Record".

About the Author

Wiktor is a prominent figure in the Polish community in the UK. He was formerly editor of the Polish monthly "Orzel Bialy", spokesman for the Federation of Poles in Great Britain and a former Ealing Councillor and has a wry detached view of life.

Lightning Source UK Ltd.
Milton Keynes UK
13 August 2010

158366UK00002B/263/P